W O W

W OMAN

OF

W ONDER

A Journey to Enlightenment

By Rehel Anderson

Rehel Anderson

I am a Spiritual Teacher and Author. My books aim to provide ways to enlighten the seeker and to attain their spiritual awakening through creativity, challenges, prayer, compassion and love. Challenges are our best teachers to help us grow more rapidly on the Journey to Enlightenment.

This is my story; this is my life. In so many ways it is no different from most. The pains, hurts, joys and moments of happiness are similar to many people. In other ways my story, my life is vastly different and many experiences are unbelievable. I would say I am as ordinary as the next person. But God gave us life and we are anything but ordinary. We all have a story to tell and not one is like the other. May you live your best life! This is mine ~ ~ ~ ~

Dedication

This book is dedicated to each of you who are seeking

Enlightenment

To keep the trust and faith needed to support your

Spiritual Journey

Acknowledgments

To my mentors – for the love, support, friendship encouragement, and never-ending belief in me.

To God – for allowing me the "challenges" I needed on my spiritual journey which continues to teach me deeper understanding, love, trust and faith.

To my special friends –

Jan - Pam - Sandy - Larry

To everyone I know that is seeking their truth.

About the Author

Rehel Anderson had many opportunities and challenges in life that made her quite unusual and interesting.

Her spirituality was a gift from God, which began around the age of seven and she had an uncanny *'knowing'* that helped her throughout her life. A *'knowing'* that most people do not attain especially at such an early age. Her *'knowing'* was the *'voice within'* which was directed by spirit and the unseen worlds. This made her life unusual, fascinating and exciting. Her spiritual journey was also of hardship, failure and triumph, but most important, she was to help others understand their journey to enlightenment

Her life was always changing with her many careers. Working at age eleven in fields planting vegetables for a local farmer, in a turkey plant, cleaning motel rooms, a waitress, office worker, secretary, television model, owner of companies, speaker for Citizens Against Crime. She held several offices in different organizations and was in the movie industry for fifteen years.

She started her movie career in the locations department, was an assistant to actors, directors, producers. She was also a double for Kim Delaney and Shirley Knight, and at the same time was a Hollywood Teamster holding a class 'A' Commercial Driver's License and became a light stunt car driver. This career was unusual as the majority of the crew members were younger and Rehel did not begin her movie career until she was age fifty and retired at age sixty-five.

With the variety of careers and no matter what life handed her, she was always guided by her spiritual side listening to the 'voice within'. Thereby she lived a life of 'duality'… career plus spirituality that governed her journey through life.

In this book you will learn many of the spiritual experiences she encountered on her journey. There are many of you who may resonate with those experiences and some of you may not understand it at all, and it cannot be explained.

Now in her later years of life, the spiritual experiences and journey continues.

Contents

The Beginning

Before being born into this earthly body, I clearly remember being on the 'other side', having full knowledge that I had lived on earth many times before, and surely did not want to experience being a human once again. I dreaded another incarnation; however, I was being summoned before the Heavenly Council. As I approached the beautiful long gold ornate table with scrolled legs that glowed with a heavenly brilliance, I saw the Heavenly Council dressed in their elegant white robes requesting me to come forward. I felt absolute peace and trust.

The Heavenly Council was directing me to incarnate back to earth one more time. Oh, how I didn't want to go back for another lifetime on earth. I wanted to stay on the 'other side' where there was so much love and peace.

The Heavenly Council presented me with a 'blueprint' for this new life's journey. It was clear that I had a choice and could say no, but I also knew that no one ever refused the Council. The main Council member had a great deal of love, compassion and understanding. He was describing my new destiny and why I was being asked to accomplish this directive one more time. I don't recall what was in the 'blueprint' for my destiny, only that I would be able to help others during my spiritual journey.

Now, leaving the peace, love and comfort of the 'other side' my life began on earth shortly before midnight October 14, 1939. My given name was Aileen DeAnne Anderson. Aileen and Kent Anderson were my very loving parents of choice while starting my new life here on earth. Aileen was very pretty with soft copper red hair and green eyes that shined when she spoke. She was very hard working and family was her priority. Kent was ever so handsome with a slender body, jet black hair and mustache. He could look like a cowboy one minute and an executive the next. He was very kind and compassionate. Along with the two loving parents, I had one bother named Gailand. He was also good looking, loved animals, outdoors and was a very gentle person. This was my perfect family to start my challenging destiny.

I was born with a distinct **'knowingness'** with a very strong **'Voice Within'.** Some would say it is an intense psychic ability. However, everyone has a Voice Within, but may not be aware of it. But as you grow in your spiritual journey you will connect with that Voice

Within. That is where you can hear the 'higher self', angels, and guides speaking to you.

Each time we return to earth, we have memories and an attachment to the *other side.* Around the age of seven, the memories begin to fade and we forget why we have come here, what we are destined to do, and what is our purpose and destiny. Then we must begin again to search for self, and attempt to find our individual purpose for life.

My spiritual journey, as I remember, began around the time I was a seven-year-old first grader. I would seek out all the different churches in our small Nevada community to learn of God and his angels. The other family members had no desire to go to church, yet I did somehow. Must have been the unseen world directing me to further my spiritual knowledge as I started my journey.

Also, at the age of seven, I had my first encounter with an extraterrestrial. Which, of course I didn't know at the time, nor had the words to express what I was experiencing.

One night while I was asleep, I thought I was having a nightmare. My mother had told me if I was having a nightmare to pinch myself, I would wake up and it would all go away. I was pinching myself frantically when what is known as a small 'grey' entered my bedroom through the wall standing at the foot of my bed…and it was not a nightmare! The small 'grey' was speaking to me telepathically, but I was so sacred all I could do was cry for my mother. As she entered my bedroom the small E.T. vanished. Mother asked me what happened. I told her there was a small, grey 'thing' with large black eyes, wearing long gray underwear standing at the foot of my bed then vanished. Not until I was in my forties, I learned that I had been observed all those years by a group of ETs. I will go into that later in the book.

We moved from that small Nevada community to a ranch in central Nevada. My father was the new foreman who took care of the ranch and thousands of cattle. He loved the cowboy lifestyle. We would sit on the top corral fence observing the beautiful night skies. We had the opportunity to experience the aurora borealis or what is known as the 'northern lights.' On another occasion while sitting on the corral fence in 1947, we watched flying saucers unaware that one of the flying saucers had crashed in Roswell, New Mexico, which became worldwide news.

We were met with many challenges while living on this ranch; however, with my loving family, they made everything seem wonderful. Our home had no electricity, or running water, no telephone, but only a battery radio to hear about the outside world.

On Christmas Eve in 1948 we drove to the nearest town to do our Christmas shopping. On our way back to the ranch some thirty miles away, it began to blizzard and the snow kept coming for days and days. We were snowed in! We could not attend school and that didn't seem important as there were only three kids in the entire school, all in the same grade, my brother, me and one other girl. It kept snowing and the temperatures had reached wind chill temperatures of 80 degrees below zero. It was so cold, frost formed on the inside walls of our bedrooms, so we had to move into the large kitchen area. That's where we lived while being snowed in from Christmas Eve 1948 until March 18, 1949.

One day we heard an airplane circling the ranch house. We couldn't imagine why an airplane would circle our house. When we ran outside and looked up, something dropped from the plane. It was a rock and tied to the rock was a small piece of cloth and a note. On the note it said, "If you are hungry eat the Hershey candy bars first." And, the note asked questions... do you need a doctor, are you sick, and with each question we were instructed to go out into the open field of snow, put our feet together and make four foot high 'yes' or 'no' answers to their questions. Once this was done, they circled the ranch house and began dropping boxes of food. Later they would come back and drop hay to the cattle as they were so hungry and cold. Most of the cattle froze to death standing up. One time when the plane circled the ranch house dropping us food, on the wing was a 100 pounds sack of flour and a large slab of bacon when it slipped off the wing near the cattle. The cattle were so hungry they ate the flour and bacon. The plane dropped us food and hay for the cattle several times during that winter. What a winter to survive!

My father made the decision to move once again. He found a job as a sheep shearer, but my mother, brother and I could not leave. If we left, there could not be a school for just one girl and we were asked to stay until the end of the school year. We could no longer live in the ranch house. What could my parents do? The only available housing was a sheep wagon, similar to the covered wagons the pilgrims traveled in. So, the sheep wagon was our home parked on the school lot until the end of the school year. When my father had time to visit us, my brother and I slept on the floor in the school house. One time when we woke up our bedding had scorpions in it. And, that was the last time we slept on the school floor.

****

Even though my immediate family was small, I had both sets of grandparents, many aunts, uncles and cousins. Whenever we had the opportunity to be in large family gatherings, we talked of loved ones who had crossed over, conversations with those loved ones, *visions* and *premonitions,* which some individuals had experienced. This ability or sensitivity appeared to be stronger in the females than the males of the family, and it was considered normal by all of us. It was never questioned. Our *knowingness* just was, and there was never any recognition of this as being psychic. The words psychic, spiritualist or medium were never uttered, because only 'crazy' people or witches were associated with those terms.

This *knowingness* was such a part of my life that, as I grew older, the *'knowingness'* grew stronger. So, I began to pay close attention to everything about me and around me. How was it that I knew so many non-specific things, or *feel* things that others didn't have a clue about? I had no doubt that someday I would acquire the answer to these questions, and what was I to do with this gift?

Around the age of twelve, my abilities were getting stronger. I knew which teachers or students liked me and who didn't like me. If I was in any danger, I was warned and knew instinctively what to do. I also knew if I put my imagination to work, whatever I dreamed or imagined would become a physical reality. This is one of the greatest tools you can learn to further your spiritual journey... called visualization. I would put it to test all the time. And, so can you.

My first test at twelve years old was to imagine or visualize one of my fantasies about boys. I imagined coming out of the house to get in my parent's car, and around the corner would come this wonderful older boy and his friend driving in a convertible, hair blowing in the wind and waving their arms at me, to jump out and excitedly say, "We've been looking for you and we finally found you". So, every day I looked down the driveway in hopes my imagined fantasy would come true. Within a month of my daydream creation, it came true exactly as I had visualized it. This young man was named Leon and became very special to me until he went into the army, and we remained friends until his passing many years later.

What I learned from this experience was, I could create whatever I would like to have in my reality by 'visualizing' it and then it would manifest. Visualizing is a great 'spiritual tool'. I recommend it!

All of my abilities and 'knowingness' seemed natural to me and thought everyone had this same ability, so it never occurred to me to discuss what I was experiencing with my mother, family or anyone until much later in life. I was experiencing wonderful things and was being taught from all of the challenges that I encountered. And, so sad that my wonderful parents never learned of my spiritual gifts or what I endured as an intuitive/psychic/medium, nor did most of the family.

My spiritual gifts were not meant to communicate with passed loved ones as some mediums do. On very rare occasions I communicated with loved ones when a person required specific information, but it is not what my gifts were meant for. I have been able to use my gifts for guidance, teaching, healing future predictions and most of all for my own learning and guidance. And, as a medium, have never charged or used my abilities as a business. It has been my special gift that I appreciate every day. And, perhaps I have helped in some small way for those who are searching for their own gifts and talents on their spiritual journey.

Atomic Bombs

Now in my early teens, our family moved to St. George, Utah where many hardships and challenges would affect my entire life.

During the 1950's our government began a project in the Nevada desert called the Test Site near Area 51. This area was where our government set off 'Atomic bombs' above ground for over 10 years to test what affects the radiation fallout from the bombs would have on the land, animals and the people. Government officials came to St. George and always informed the town's people that there was nothing to be concerned about. This was our government, so why would anyone not believe what they had been told.

The town's people were excited to have this different experience and to observe the bombs when they were detonated 120 miles away at the Nevada Test Site. The school would take different classes by bus to the top of the mountain to watch the bombs when they were detonated. On the day of the largest bomb detonation called 'Dirty Harry' the 10th grade class was taken to the top of the mountain to watch the huge bomb blast. Shortly after the explosion the winds came filled with light sand mixed with a light rain. As the wind came it was so hot, it gave the students an instant like sunburn. One student reached for the top of her head and as she did, her entire scalp came off and her face was totally burned. She became very ill and months later she was taken to California for medical care. The doctors were not educated how to treat patients with radiation burns. They tried experimental injections into her face, she developed polio and at one point the doctors said she was terminal. Many different kinds of illnesses affected thousands of people that were exposed to the radiation. The largest percentage of health issues were cancer and thyroid problems.

Years later we started a 'class action law suit' against the government. However, not all health conditions were accepted in the law suit. If a person died of cancer, it must be only a 'certain' type of cancer. Hundreds of people had thyroid disease and the government was not concerned about other types of diseases or conditions someone was suffering from.

The young girl that was so affected during that 'bomb watching' outing was still alive twenty-seven years later when our 'class action' law suit went to court. Her hair never grew back and her face was a yellow/green after the injections the doctors had used as an attempt to save the skin on her face.

I have had many health issues my entire life from the exposure to the radiation. At age thirty-seven doctors diagnosed me with tumors in my head. When I had the surgery to remove three tumors, the tumors where not a 'normal' type tumor. They were 'radiated' balls of sand which looked like a regular type tumor. The sand came from the wind and the light rain when they detonated the bombs, which I breathed in. It took all those years to form these strange tumors in my head. Other friends developed the radiated balls of sand in their breasts, which had to be removed, and many had pregnancy issues.

We did not win the law suit however some farmers were paid for the loss of sheep and some were paid a small amount of money. During that time one of our prominent attorneys was Congressman Stewart Udall from Arizona.

Fifty years after the law suit during President Clinton's term, the government allocated money to be paid to the families that were named in the class action law suit. However, President Clinton instead of allocating the money for all of the law suit victims allocated the money for the Parks & Recreation Department. And, no monies that I know of were paid to any of those families. I never received any for my health issues.

The results of the bomb testing were unimaginable. Thousands of sheep, cattle, birds and people died. The land was radiated and crops were destroyed. In our small community over fifteen hundred people died of cancer, thyroid diseases and much more. I lost my dear mother from cancer due to the huge amounts of radiation she was exposed to while working in the garden on the day of 'Dirty Harry'. It left a horrible burn on her back as if she had been burned with an iron. My father had a radiation burn on his nose that didn't heal for twenty-nine years.

Fifty years later, the government asked me to be tested for one year to see why I had lived and had not died as so many others. They were unable to find any reason why I lived, or that is what I was told. My belief is that God had a bigger plan for me. All the people throughout Utah and adjoining states that are still alive have serious health issues. We are called 'Downwinders'. The reason we are called 'Downwinders' is the government waited until the wind would blow to the East where it wouldn't affect as many people They wanted to make sure the wind would not blow towards Las Vegas or Los Angeles or any community that was highly populated.

In 1954, John Wayne, Susan Hayward, Dick Powell and many crew members were exposed to the radiation while filming the movie 'The Conqueror' and later died of cancer because of the radiation exposure. I also spent time with John Wayne and those actors during that time. Fortunately, John Wayne's son (Patrick Wayne) was the first to expose the consequences of radiation poisoning in Utah. He also created the John Wayne Cancer Insurance for anyone that wanted cancer insurance. John Wayne died of cancer from radiation, and did not die because he was a smoker as the news reported.

We have learned that radiation never goes away, and affects people for generations.

John Wayne & Rehel - 1954

Filming the movie: The Conqueror

15

During the time we lived in St. George, I was married (at a very young age) to a city policeman. We had two boys that were born with health issues because of the radiation in my body and, as adults, they have their own children which has affected them as well.

Also, at this time I felt a 'spiritual void' as my 'knowingness' or 'voice within' was silent. Was it because of radiation exposure or was it the unhappy marriage I had jumped into and divorced five years later, or was I just off track from my destiny? How was I to know?

Obviously, this new life journey I had agreed upon would become a rocky one and it appeared that my 'blueprint' was not going to be an easy one this time around.

Coming Back

Soon after my divorce I became aware that my intuitive ability was coming back to life. I now lived in Salt Lake City and began to pay full attention to the *knowingness* that I was developing rapidly in my mind. I could tell in advance who was calling on the phone, who would be lying to me and why, what problems were in store for me or others around me.

One day at work some girls invited me to go with them for a 'psychic' reading. I always wanted to experience a psychic reader, yet deep inside I felt somewhat afraid. The moment had arrived and my heart was beating ninety miles an hour. Henrietta was her name, opened the door with a big warm smile. She seemed to be very kind and I studied how different she appeared. She was very thin, had bright red hair, her eyes were the eyes of a cat, in shape and color. She was dressed in bright yellow and, cat like, tossed her head up and down. She also had a calmness about her that took away my nervousness. I was excited about my reading and it sounded very good. She told me I would marry a man much older than myself, he would have money, and he would be different than anyone I had ever dated. He would adopt my boys, we would move to another state, and travel to foreign countries. I enjoyed this new experience, although I was still quite skeptical. I decided to withhold my judgment until the results were in.

I believe all humans have some psychic ability, whether it has been developed or not, and animals, domesticated or wild have psychic/intuitive awareness as well. I was fortunate that Henrietta was a 'good' psychic. Not all psychics are as well developed or truthful. After this experience I became more enthusiastic about my own developing abilities. I paid close attention to my feelings and premonitions as they became clearer to me as time passed.

I was tired and discouraged taking care of my boys and not being able to give them all the things that they deserved. I asked God to send me a man with money to help me with my struggles. That was my desire.

I remarried a year or so later and the gist of Henrietta's reading came back to me. She had predicted I would marry a man much older than I. He would be financially well off, move to another state, we would travel to foreign countries; he would adopt my boys, and would be like no one I had ever dated before. And, sure enough all that she predicted was the man I just married.

I hadn't learned yet that when you ask God or the universe for something you really need to be specific. I had asked God to bring me a man with money, but I forgot to ask for the qualifications that I would like, such as his character. He was a powerful business man that had many dealings with some very shady people, and was not honest or trust worthy. This marriage lasted five years for I knew there was more to life. I'm also a firm believer that no matter what choices we make, there are beneficial lessons to be gained from all of our choices, good and bad, and it is also part of our 'blueprint' of life. Sometimes the good is hard to recognize because it is accompanied by tough times. But each challenge makes you stronger and hopefully you learn from them.

Premonitions

It was a glorious beautiful day in April. The children were playing outdoors when I had an overwhelming feeling that something was wrong or going to be wrong. I listened and tried to pay attention to what I was *feeling*. The *thought* and *feeling* came to me that I must gather my boys quickly and take them to see my grandmother (their great-grandmother) for this would be the last time we would see her. The urgency was almost unbearable and I *knew* I had to go to grandma's house right away.

When we arrived at her house, she was very surprised to see us and wondered why we had come for a visit since it was not our normal time to visit. I merely said I wanted to see her before we moved to Las Vegas the next week.

As we sat enjoying each other's company, she talked of my cousins wedding that would be coming up in the next few weeks. She made a statement "I'm not sure I'll be here to attend Linda's wedding, but I hope so."

I asked her, "Grandma, where do you think you will be going if you don't go to the wedding?"

She kept repeating, "I'm not sure, but I just don't think I will be here."

I had such a sinking feeling and I also wondered how correct my premonition was. Was this going to be the last time I saw my grandmother or was I just feeling a sense of loss since we were moving the following week?

I kept going back into my thoughts about another faint premonition I was having, but it was not as clear as the one of my Grandmother. During the day, I would get the *feeling* that I was going to lose my mother or my father and one of them would be living with me. I would question, "Is this my mother or is this my father?" I couldn't get a clear picture or answer. Was this something else I needed to pay attention to?

My husband, children and I moved to Las Vegas the next week where we settled into our new life. Then the dreadful day came with the phone call that you don't want to hear, "I'm sorry, Grandma passed away the day after Linda's wedding." Yes, that confirmed my premonition. How did Grandma know? How do any of *us* know when it is our time?

A short time after that I took another trip to visit the family. My mother, her sister (my aunt) and I spent the day together. My aunt became upset over some visions she was having where she would see my grandmother floating on a cloud trying to tell her something and thought she might die soon, however, my mother assured her that it was not true. I was paying close attention as it seemed my premonitions concerned the death of loved ones.

I returned to Las Vegas and life became normal for a short while until the day I received another dreaded phone call. My dad was telling me that my mother was very ill and I should come home. My premonition of losing my mother or my father now told me it would be my beloved mother. My mother had never been sick so what was wrong? The doctors informed me she had cancer and only had eleven months to live. How could this be? She was only forty-six years old!

She tried so hard to get well and endured the many medical treatments to make her more comfortable. We were informed that the huge amounts of radiation from the Atomic bombs she had been exposed to caused her cancer. Our government used us as Guinea pigs to test the Atomic bombs. How dare they put our lives in jeopardy??

The last month of her life she had gone into a deep coma and the family asked someone from the church to come pray for her. When the gentlemen arrived, as they walked into her hospital room, my dear mother woke from her coma and said, "I've been waiting for you." She looked at me and said, "It's going to be alright." Then she closed her eyes and received a wonderful last prayer. When the prayer ended, she opened her eyes, thanked them for coming, looked at me and repeated, "It's going to be alright," and drifted back into her deep coma.

Several days and nights went by and then one evening I was informed it would be only a matter of minutes before she would pass away. There were about twenty family members in the room. My uncle was holding her right hand. I was on her left side leaning against the wall and for whatever reason I started saying the Lord's Prayer to myself. This was strange for I had fallen away from all churches long ago.

And, now, the most wonderful, glorious, loving experience of my life was about to happen. I looked up to the ceiling over my mother's head, and out of the ceiling came my deceased grandmother and a man I did not recognize. They were not in full body, but I saw them from the waist to the top of their heads. The man said nothing; then my grandmother spoke.

"Come on Aileen, we have to go."

My mother didn't move and I kept staring in awe. Then my grandmother in a very stern voice said again, "Come on Aileen, we have to go!"

As soon as she spoke those words, I heard my mother's voice (in my head) in a very weak and drawn-out voice say, "I'm hurrying as fast as I can." I looked down towards her feet and witnessed her *spirit* move from the tips of her toes up through her entire body and her spirit departed out the center of her forehead. The three of them left – though the ceiling – departing to the other side.

The most wonderful feeling of an indescribable love swept over me, yet there was the sadness and grief of losing my beloved mother. Did anyone in the room witness this expression of life and death, a transition that obviously takes place when we leave this plane of existence? Our physical body dies, but we live on in spirit and we are not alone when it is our time to cross over.

Learning that no one in the room witnessed this transition, I thanked God for this gift to see life and death. Shortly after my mother's passing my father did live with me for a while as my premonition had suggested.

****

My life was changing rapidly. I was divorced again and had to make a new beginning for myself and my boys once again.

I was working at a hotel in Las Vegas, had a new boyfriend and life was running smoothly. Then as nice as it was, disturbing feelings mounted in me. What was it? My boyfriend was leaving for Costa Rica the following day, but I wasn't concerned about that. But, on this particular day while at work I was going through many emotions that I could not figure out. It started with a sinking feeling; I became fidgety, then angry, and at times giggled and acted silly, then despair hit me. I just could not pull myself together and finally it was time to go home.

My boyfriend and I had planned to have dinner before his trip to Costa Rica. I was not in any stable mood to fix dinner so went outside and paced back and forth around the swimming pool while he fixed dinner. Then the dreaded phone call came - once again- on the other end was my sister-in-law who didn't say anything other than "Gailand is dead." We were like twins; born so close together we were in the same grade in school, now killed in a tremendous freak truck accident at the age of thirty-three. Instantly I *knew* what had entangled my emotions that day. God and my brother had been calling out to me one more time.

Again, another phenomenon happened. At the funeral before the casket is closed it is our family custom to pass by the casket and say our last goodbyes. I walked to the head of the casket, leaned over to kiss my brother on the forehead. As I did, he shook his head back and forth as if to say "No don't do that." I was jarred and stunned while some people made this comment. "I thought I saw Gailand's head move." Yes, it did, and he had not yet gone to the other side, and perhaps did not realize he had been killed in that dreadful freak truck accident.

Health Issues

The rein of sadness had finally let up and I was continuing my normal daily life trying to work and raise my sons. During the next few years, I had many struggles with my own health. I seemed to encounter such odd symptoms and strange diseases that doctors could not explain. At times I had x-rays and blood tests that gave one diagnosis and the next time they gave a completely different diagnosis. What was this all about? Some doctors suspected it was being exposed to all the radiation from the Atomic Bombs.

One time a few days before Thanksgiving I had trouble with my legs and it was difficult to walk or move. I was to spend Thanksgiving with my father and other family members in Salt Lake City, but before I left I called the doctor and asked if he could get me a pair of crutches as I needed support to walk. This alarmed the doctor and requested that I go to the hospital immediately. After I put the boys on the airplane I checked into the hospital

A group of doctors put me through several tests to determine a diagnosis, yet they had none. One day as I was laying in my hospital bed a group of doctors came in to give me the bad news. This is what was said, "I'm sorry but your paralysis is not just affecting your legs, it is moving up through your body. Once it gets above the waist, it will affect all of your upper body and you will be in an iron lung, probably the rest of your life."

Instantly I began to laugh. The doctors could not figure out why I was laughing and repeated how serious this condition was. And, at that moment a *very strong* and *powerful* thought ran through my mind, "I have two boys to take care of, I live in a two-story house, this will not happen!" The doctors had nothing else to say and left with puzzlement on their faces.

The wonderful part of this story is, a few days later I was released from the hospital, walked the best I could without help, went home and took care of all my responsibilities. So, what happened? I know that God healed me and gave me the power to help heal myself. Can I explain how it happened? No, but I just know there was a gift of healing… from GOD to me.

****

Life was finally normal again; working and having fun. Dancing was my favorite past time. I could dance the night away and all troubling matters would be gone.

One night my friend Lil asked me to go dancing at a country western club. We danced every dance until we had to sit down and rest for a while. She invited her dance partner to sit with us to get better acquainted. He suggested I would be interested in his friend that would be arriving soon. Oh no, I thought…this is not the kind of man I was ever interested in and my intention was just to dance the night away with no interference.

Well, the next phenomenon was about to happen in my life. The friend did arrive and walked slowly up to the table and was introduced to us one by one, and while hellos were being said, I heard this *thought* or *voice* say, *"You are going to marry this man."*

I started to scream inside my own head, "No, no, not this man, please not this man. He doesn't interest me, and he's not even my type."

I couldn't imagine why the spirit world wanted me to marry this man. He was a dealer in a hotel casino, been in and out of drugs, was a loan shark, had dealings with the underworld, and had been in prison. Then, you guessed it, a few short months later we were married. He watched ball games endlessly on television with my sons and his shady side was not evident in any way. Then it became obvious why God had put him in my life.

I had become very ill. The doctors found three growths in my head. I was losing my memory, became weak, stressful and lost weight. Surgery was the only possible way to get well. So, God sent me a man that was kind, considerate and peaceful, who acted as a father to my sons, and he became the best nurse I would need during this trying time.

The surgery was scheduled for November and I started to have '*feelings*' that I was not going to make it. Was I going to die? I was not afraid but determined to get everything in my life in order. The only thing I was unable to do was tell my father. He had gone through so much and he couldn't bear it if something happened to me.

The day before surgery my '*thoughts*' began to change. The *voice* or *thought* said, "It's going to be okay." I questioned, "Why did I have the feeling that I was going to die and now I'm told it's going to be okay. I don't understand." I had no answer.

The day of surgery, I remember it was November and still don't remember if it was 1977 or 1978. I do remember being prepped for surgery, I remember being in the operating room, I remember the anesthetic being injected into me. Then, I remember *falling* and suddenly everything went *pitch black* and a *black wall appeared* – I was gone!

I know you have heard stories of people having 'out of body experiences' or 'near death' experiences while being in the operating room where they leave their body and are able to look down and see what everyone is doing. No, this did not happen to me. It was much stranger. I hit that black wall and became a different person *physically* and *mentally*.

When I became conscious several hours later, my head was as big as a basketball. I couldn't recognize myself and only remember the first couple of days in the hospital. Amnesia had set in. I don't know how long I was in that state. However, I do remember the day my consciousness/memory came back. I was in the shower; I was in a panic because I did not know what the water was or how to get out of the strange enclosure. All of a sudden, my mind knew I was in the shower and I could open the door to the shower. My mind came back into the present time in a flash.

It was always a mystery to me. How did my brain know that I didn't know, and how did my brain let me know what I was doing in the shower when I was so afraid before I came out of amnesia? Our brains are truly amazing! The three tumors removed from my head were 'radiated balls of sand' which had formed because of my breathing in the light, moist sand during the Atomic bomb detonations.

As time went on, we all thought that I would begin to look more like myself, and slowly I did, but I had changed. The 'old me' was a lot more attractive, flirtatious, sensual, exciting, out-going, slim and quite into ones-self, this 'new' me was not any of those things anymore.

I no longer had amnesia, but had little memory. The doctors suggested I take some type of schooling to gain back 'memory retention'. I took a real estate course which I passed but was still too ill to pursue any type of work.

I tried to recapture so many memories. I thought about my marriages, children, family, jobs, friends, places I had lived and I couldn't imagine this had been my life. It seemed as though I had read a book of experiences about someone else's life. Not mine. I had no *personal attachment or feelings* to those memories. When people would tell me stories of what we had done together, I had absolutely no recall of what they were telling me. Why couldn't I remember? I thought this must be how a person feels when they go through the 'government witness protection program'. They have to learn a new identity. Was I a new identity and where was the old 'me'?

In time I did physically look more like me, but did not have the same personality. I was now more introverted, had a lot more compassion, love, patience and understanding than the old me.

Walk-In

I learned of people with similar stories. These people are called **'walk-ins'**. Could I be? Is this what I had become? How would I ever find out?

A **walk-in** experience will generally take two forms. The **'number one'** most **common** walk-in is when another 'soul is integrated with' that person's own body, soul, spirit, energy and higher self to assist with the distress and trauma the individual can't cope with any longer. The 'walk-in' will assist in the person's destiny or until the walk-in is no longer needed. Then that 'walk-in' will **'walk-out'** if the person is able to continue their destiny without assistance.

The **second** most **'uncommon' walk-in** is when an actual *'new soul, spirit* & consciousness' transfers into and inhabits a person's body while the *original soul & spirit* of that person departs their physical body and the earth plane. The new soul, spirit & consciousness, now lives in the human body of the person that departed and will usually carry out the life path or destiny of the person that departed. And, in some unique cases during the life time of that body/vehicle, there can be three or

34

more soul transferences before that physical body dies. The physical body is used by the spirit world.

Again, the physical body looks similar, but the personality changes and the new soul observes the memories and the past of the person that departed, but does not have any emotional attachment to those memories. As explained before, similar to a person being in the government witness program. And in this case, the individual's soul and spirit went to the other side permitting the new soul to take over the physical body. It does not happen without a previous mutual agreement while on the other side prior to a new lifetime.

As we have gone into the new millennium, many more 'separate' soul transferences are taking place. This is occurring because our planet has become so full of negative energy, and more enlightened souls are coming to help balance the energy, bringing more love and peace. These individuals are the light workers you hear about. These souls are placed in bodies who have different professions and lived in different countries throughout the planet to help build up the planet's energy. They are here to assist in the upcoming future events. Some light workers are recognized while others in political and high-powered positions are not recognized.

Yes, this is what happened to me! I became a **walk-in** of the **first kind.**

****

Within two months of the surgery, I was obsessed to learn all about the psychic world. I attended every group, meeting, lecture, and read only the books I was directed to read. That was my life! I practiced every day subjects I had been taught. All the *gifts-talents-knowing* I had when I was younger were amplified ten times over.

Three years after the surgery, the 'gentle man' that God had put in my life was now out of my life as quickly as he had arrived as I was unable to accept his life style, yet, I knew God placed him in my life to help me during that challenging period. We remained friends until he passed away.

My health improved greatly and I was able to work and settle into a more normal lifestyle.

****

Several years had gone by; my sons were both happily married with children. I was devoted to learning about the 'spirit world' and the 'unknown'. I went to as many places and met as many spiritual people as I could. At times I felt some of these experiences were quite ridiculous, but I kept at it until I found the people and the compatibility I was looking for. That's where I met my 'mentor' Tom Hart; a born psychic originally from New York who started giving readings at age five. He had the greatest way of teaching people how to get rid of their superstitions, fears, and misconceptions. To teach them *'who they really are'* and what our lives and destiny's mean. He explained the difference between a psychic and a spiritualist.

Psychics have the ability to talk with the dead, have the ability to find ghosts, give card readings, those that assist police departments to find the missing or dead, and much more.

A spiritualist contacts and communicates with the universal spirit world, the Souls, Masters, space brothers, and is always connected with God and religion.

I'm sure you have heard this expression, **"when you pray, you talk to God, when you meditate, God talks to you."** That is the Voice Within! Most of us have a *feeling* or *premonition,* but don't *hear* the *thoughts* or *words* or *see* the *visions* that the **Voice Within** is passing on to us.

I had learned to meditate and now my meditation was a strict routine every evening starting at 11:00 PM for one hour. This is the most valuable lesson for anyone, for meditation brings the ability to 'listen' to the **Voice Within!**

I was also practicing 'treasure mapping' or some people call it a 'vision board' where you make a list with pictures of all the things you are asking the spirit world for. I asked the spirit world for a new house, a new job, a new man and a new Lincoln.

That's exactly what I got in a very short time – a new house, a new job and a man in my life named 'Lincoln'. I forgot to be *specific* what I was asking for - I did not specify that the Lincoln was an 'automobile'. So, the spirit world gave me a man *named* Lincoln! I learned quickly we must be specific in what we are asking for.

Tom, our mentor, formed a small spiritual group and held meetings twice a week. In our group was, Cecilia a nurse anesthetist, Lincoln a security guard for Elvis Presley, Dean retained conscious memories of his previous lifetime, Delores a school principal, Larry a computer analyst and me, the channel/medium.

At first, we had an open-door policy for anyone that wanted to attend our group. Dozens came and went, even some well-known and famous people, until the spirit world gave us instructions what was expected of us if we wanted to advance in the spirit world. We were given the reason that not all people are on the same level of spiritual advancement and each individual has a different energy frequency and color code. We were given the analogy that a student in the twelfth grade does not spend time in the second grade and the second grader does not spend time in the twelfth grade if they are not ready.

We did as spirit asked and felt our small intimate group was on the same level of advancement. Also, the spirit world informed us when it was allowed to bring outsiders into our group for special occasions.

The first night with our select group, Tom said to the spirit world, "I think there are twelve of you spirits with us tonight, is that right"? Immediately the answer came back. "No, there are fifty-six of us." They did not want us to ask their names as it was unimportant, but they would call us the 'yellow circle', and I as the medium/spiritualist/healer was to be known as 'The Little One'. Also, when we advanced in our learning and understanding of the spirit world, we would advance into a different higher 'color code'. We were asked not to read many books, as much of what is written is misinformation and they would teach us from the universal records. However, if a book appeared from out of nowhere or was presented out of some unusual circumstance, then it was meant to be read to help in the process.

As the trance medium/spiritualist/healer, I was to *communicate* for the spirit world. We were being taught from the fifty-six different spirits, all with different information. As we advanced into greater understanding, we were taught from some of the Masters, and then we were able to connect with 'Source'. When we had special meetings for outsiders, and those outsiders wanted information we were given the most highly qualified Spirits/Souls/Masters or the 'Source' that would supply them the right/truthful answers. We had doctors, engineers, scientists and more visit our meetings to gain knowledge imparted to them from the universe.

On one special occasion Norman and June (his wife) came to our meeting. Norman had cancer and Dean wanted to help him. Norman was Jewish, was terminal, all funeral arrangements were made days earlier. At this special meeting Norman was given a healing. After leaving the meeting he became very ill. He vomited a black fluid for several days, and his hair and beard rapidly turned white. He was schedule for a bone marrow test which was very painful. He called and asked if I could assist in any way. I prayed to God that

Norman would not have a painful test, to shower him with love and bring a healing to this very ill man. After his bone marrow test, Norman came driving very quickly into my drive way, jumped out of the car and yelled, "There was no pain, there was no pain!" Later the doctors could not find one sign of cancer in Norman. Thank you, God for the healing! Completely healed he and his wife moved to North Carolina and opened a gym.

In some of the earlier stages of learning from the spirit world, I had skepticism and disbelief about myself. I had such doubt this could be me or what was happening to me. I just knew *anyone* could do the same thing. I doubted so much this special gift was taken from me. I could not use 'the voice' as a medium, but we faithfully conducted our meetings every week. Without the voice, the spirit world used my body to communicate. At times my body would be suspended over the back of a chair as rigid as a log. Other times my body would be in great contortions and I knew I was not able to do this on any conscious level. I could use 'sign language' to communicate to the group, and they did their best to figure out what was being said. As much as I wanted to hear the voice within again there was no verbal spiritual messages for one long month. Once I learned the value of this gift and how to use and respect it, the spirit world returned the gift of verbal communication or channeling

41

back to me. I realized as a spiritualist I was to serve in the best possible way from then on and never doubt or take advantage of this gift.

During those years with our special group, I met Olof Jonsson, one of the world's leading psychics. Olof worked with our government and Edgar Mitchell when Mitchell was on Apollo 14 to test ESP. He was hired by Mel Fisher to find the huge treasure that was on the shipwrecked Atocha. He was also hired by Ferdinand Marcos to find the Japanese gold hidden in the Philippines. However, Olof left and did not disclose where the gold was hidden as he knew Marcos was going to have him assassinated once the treasure was discovered. Olof became my friend and mentor. He taught me physical healing, mental telepathy, move objects with my mind, levitation, teleport objects, about bi-location and bio-location, and how to call in the space craft with our space brothers, and much more. I am sorry to say Olof died in 1998 at the age of 79.

Rehel   Lincoln   Olof

I was able to communicate with the universal spirits, our space brothers, entities, departed loved ones, angels, and the highest of all communications called the 'Source' and sometimes known as the 'Force' which is energy or power, that has never been in body or ever will be. The 'Source' does not have a name or wished to be named. The 'Source' desires to inter-act with our souls, hearts and minds, and for all of us to speak our truth and to understand that truth.

Space Brothers

In what we consider the "UFO" world, I am known as a 'contactee'. As I mentioned before, my first contact was at the age of seven when the little grey alien came into my bedroom and disappeared when my mother entered. I was observed for over 40 years before any communication began.

A contactee is different than an 'abductee'. A contactee is a person who has mental communications (telepathy) with our space brothers and is given information about earth, earth conditions, possible future events, explanations of space, universes, and much more.

An 'abductee' is a person who is abducted in their physical body and taken on board a space craft or some other location. They are physically examined, implanted with devices and endured frightening experiences. Whitley Strieber, author of 'Communion' was abducted with terrifying experiences. Betty and Barney Hill are the first legitimate and most investigated couple who encountered a space craft. They were terrified, taken aboard to be examined and then returned to their location.

I've had many telepathic communications with our 'space brothers'. They shared information about the universe, their role with planet earth, the different types of 'aliens' and answered many questions that most of us have. They surround us all the time to watch what we are doing to our planet and our civilizations. They will not intervene unless we cause destruction that would affect the other planets or universes. They 'project' or 'implant' information and technology into minds of people like Steve Jobs, Tesla, Einstein, Elon Musk and many leaders of countries, and to create new inventions which will be of benefit to our world. They are monitoring our climate around the planet and when anything goes too far out of control, they will intervene. They have selected many people around the globe to communicate (like me) and are given instructions what to do in the future so the public will not be afraid, and to understand their purpose for our planet. Fortunately, all of my communications with our space brothers have been very positive, informative and I have had nothing to fear.

During the years we conducted our spiritual group I became friends with Robert (Bob) Achzehner. He was in charge of the Aerial Phenomenon Research Organization. At one time, he helped investigate the UFO that crashed near Roswell, New Mexico in 1947, and was fortunate enough to have obtained a small piece of the craft. While attending our group, he had each one of us hold the metal like material, which immediately returned to its shape after we wadded it up in our hands. And, it certainly was not a piece of a weather balloon as the government wanted the public to believe!

BOB ACHZEHNER
Aerial Phenomenon Research
Organization

UFO Conference

In one of our weekly spiritual meetings the space brothers communicated with us and said I was to go the UFO Conference in Laramie, Wyoming. I was to purchase a 'special light' similar to a black light, go to the conference and there I was to scan the bodies of the attendees. While scanning the bodies, if there were white spots on their bodies it would confirm these individuals were either contacted or abducted by the extraterrestrials.

The UFO Conference was at the University of Wyoming conducted by Dr. Leo Sprinkle. Since I had met Dr. Sprinkle at previous conferences, I called and informed him of the plan. Dr. Sprinkle arranged time during the conference for attendees to be scanned if they wished. This was exciting as only one person did not have white spots on them, which meant everyone at the conference at one time or another had been visited by an extraterrestrial. And, the most interesting scan was a woman with her eleven-year-old son that had identical white spots on their bodies and not like any other person.

Because this was such a success, Dr. Sprinkle asked me to come back the next year. And, much to our surprise – not one person attending the conference had any white spots on them. Dr. Sprinkle informed me he learned once the public learns how to scan and to confirm humans have been visited by E.T.'s, the E.T.'s will change the discovery and it will no longer be valid.

The same year I was privileged to be interviewed and tested by the well-known John Mack who investigated many people that had UFO sightings, been contacted or abducted by our space brothers.

The final year I attended the Conference, I was driving from Salt Lake City to Laramie. Shortly before arriving in Laramie, I felt something was wrong with the steering or front end of the car. The weekend coming up was the 4th of July and all repair shops would be closed for the holiday. I decided after our morning break I would go to the car dealership to get it repaired. The service manager at the Lincoln dealership said they were too busy, but could refer me to another mechanic across town. I became quite agitated when I looked into the service bays and not one car was being repaired. Without arguing I decided to drive very carefully to the mechanic across town.

I explained to the next service manager the problems I was having with the car and that I needed to drive back to Salt Lake City right after the conference. Now, I was almost in a state of shock. He said he was sorry, but was too busy. Not one car was in the service bay being repaired. What was going on?

I went back to the conference fretting when Dr. Sprinkle assured me his mechanic could repair my car. He would call him at our lunch break to make arrangements. Problem solved or so I thought!

I was very engrossed in the conference, when I *heard thoughts,* and *saw a vision in my head* that said, "Take your car on this road to the place we are showing you, and please go alone and tell no one."

We broke for lunch. I excused myself and drove on the road that I had never been on before. I kept driving and looking for the area that I was shown in my head. Finally, I could see it, but I could not find a road to get there. I tried every road I came to and just couldn't get to the location, so I decided to turn around and go back to the conference. As I was driving back, out of the corner of my right eye, I caught a glimpse of a dirt road. Was this the road I was to take? "Could be, I thought, but I'll just go back to town."

At that moment, the *voice* promptly said, "Turn around." I immediately turned around and drove up the dirt road until I came to a plateau. There was nothing but sagebrush, gravel and weeds. Then I *heard,* "Stop, get out of the car and walk in a circle and don't go near the green bush."

49

There was a small green bush not more than ten or twelve inches high. I started to walk in a circle with the green bush in the center of my circle. I kept walking and walking and heard nothing. I thought, "Boy, if anyone sees me, they are going to think I'm stark raving crazy, and I'm not too sure of it myself."

I walked in that circle for about twenty minutes and in the distance, I saw a motorcycle coming in my direction and became concerned for my safety. I was a female, alone, in the desert, and a long way from town. I wondered what would happen if I stayed much longer. Then I heard in my head, "Get in your car and leave."

I was relieved, got in the car and quickly headed back to town. I left the dirt road and turned onto the paved highway when I *heard,* "Stop at the Subway Sandwich shop, have a half tuna fish sandwich and a coke. Go back to the conference, and, oh by the way, your car is fixed."

Wow, my car was fixed and lunch was ordered. How good was that? And, better yet, I never had another mechanical problem with my car and sold it several years later. I was so grateful for the *voice within and/or* the 'space mechanics' no matter what or who did the repairs!! And, it also taught me that the unseen world is always around to help me when needed.

****

Even though I had many communications with the 'space brothers' I questioned how true much of it had been. I was always questioning, doubting and arguing, but never fully letting go of old beliefs I had grown up with. There weren't aliens or space ships, was there? I decided I didn't want any more *contact* with them unless I could *see* them in their 'physical being' and to know that it was not a trick of my mind. I always need proof or evidence of some kind no matter who I receive information from, and I wanted confirmation. I thought if I could see them physically, then I would have the real answers to my questions.

I spoke sternly into space hoping the space brothers would hear me. "I don't want you to contact me anymore. I want to see you in the physical or not at all, I've had enough" I said.

That night I went to bed expecting not to be disturbed when woken up by someone sitting on the end of my bed. I was startled as there was only an indentation as if someone was sitting there, but whoever, whatever was there was invisible. Suddenly I was in space, flying, zooming, powered by some force or energy at great speed. I was in a craft and saw no one. The craft was very dark almost like a dark/blue/black color. I saw no instruments, dials, seats, but only saw a small rectangular window that I could look out. I couldn't imagine where I was. Then a beautiful deep male voice spoke to me.

"You are here."

That started my defenses. Speaking sternly, I said, "I know I am home in bed how can I be here?"

"Yes, you are here and in bed."

"How can I be home in bed and here too?"

"It is called *bi-location*"

"If I am here, where am I?"

"You are directly over Calville Bay."

Calville Bay is a recreation area on Lake Mead near Las Vegas, which is used for boaters to launch their boats and other recreations.

The voice began to tell me the most wondrous information that was going to happen, to myself, to people I knew, the world, and so much more. I became so excited I could hardly contain myself.

I asked why this was such a secret, and that *"they"* or I or someone in authority needed to inform everyone what they just told me. And when I suggested this to the voice, he said, "Yes, you may tell of this experience to anyone you choose, but the information we've given you will be stricken from your mind, *until it's time.*"

And, at that moment this wondrous information was stricken from my mind and I only remember my experience as I have related it to you.

The 'space brothers' did leave me alone and three years later in the middle of the night, that deep beautiful '*voice*' returned and simply said, "*It's almost time*", and again six years later in the night that beautiful voice said, "*It's almost time,*" and again a few years later. I always wondered when '*It's time*' is going to be. And, I was never given the opportunity to see them in the physical…yet!

However, years later while taking an afternoon nap in a hotel in California I was awakened by the *voice within* that said, "Walk out on the patio, look up in the sky." To my amazement, there in the sky was a space craft not like any I had seen before or since. This craft was 'barrel' shaped, tan in color, similar to a very large barrel of oil. I watched it as it slowly moved from west to east across the entire Los Angeles valley. Even though we stopped communicating, I had proof they are still around me and just waiting for me to communicate once again.

****

During the 80's I met a man named Harry. He was the best friend of George Van Tassel. George Van Tassel was interested in Nickola Tesla's research for electromagnetic energy and worked for and was a friend of Howard Hughes. Van Tassel was well known for communicating with extraterrestrials. He built a huge 'underground' facility at Giant Rock near Joshua Tree, California where he installed technical equipment in order to reach and communicate with our alien brothers, as I call them. All of his communications with the E.T.'s was recorded. Harry gave me some of those recordings which I still have. In those recordings George was told how the aliens helped to create earth. They brought us the first flower, which was a rose, brought the almond, the pomegranate and more.

George was instructed to build what is known as the 'Integratron'. The building would create anti-gravity and electromagnetic energy and sound frequencies. The purpose was to rejuvenate human cells so one could look younger and live longer. He built the Integratron as instructed without using any nails and only used some glue.

During the many years communicating with E.T.'s at Giant Rock, he would hold huge outdoor UFO conferences. At one of those conferences over five thousand people attended. Many police officers and highway patrol directed the traffic. It was when people used the Polaroid camera. A highway patrolman took a picture with his Polaroid camera of the crowd and Giant Rock. It takes a few minutes for the Polaroid to develop the picture and much to his surprise there was a space craft in the picture which no one was able to see with the naked eye.

It was learned that President Dwight D. Eisenhower had a 'secret' visit at Giant Rock, met with George Van Tassel, communicated with the extraterrestrials and was given valuable information.

My friend, Harry, George Van Tassel's best friend related this story to me.

Sometime after President Eisenhower visited Giant Rock, George felt he was having a heart attack when suddenly he was encountered by three 'men in black' who took him by ambulance to the hospital and refused to let George's wife ride with them. After she arrived at the hospital one of the men asked her to identify George's body as he had died. They took her to an area to identify George, but when they raised the sheet above his head, it *was not* George's body. She was

55

threatened and told the same thing would happen to her, so at some point she had to agree that it was her husband George. No one ever knew the truth of what happened to George. The propaganda records say that George was in a hotel in Santa Ana, California and died of a heart attack. My friend, Harry, said that was absolutely not the truth. Immediately the government came and destroyed the Giant Rock facility and filled it with dirt. All of George's papers and records of any kind disappeared.

Because of this incident, my friend Harry was afraid for his life and disappeared for several years. After I met Harry, I begged him to take me to Giant Rock.

Harry finally relented and took Lincoln and me to Giant Rock. Giant Rock had been destroyed and taken over by drug gangs, however, after all these years you can now visit that area and take a tour.

While at Giant Rock we were able to experience the incredible energy frequencies of the Integratron. I stood on the second floor directly under the dome opening in an area about eighteen inches square. When I spoke, the sound would boom as if being on a loud speaker. As soon as I took one step out of the eighteen- inch square, my voice was very very quiet. Amazing!

George   Van   Tassel

Harry – Giant Rock – Integratron
Yucca Valley, California

In the 80's there were five 'silver balls' found in certain areas around the world. One ball was found on a plateau in the California desert several miles East of Giant Rock. The silver ball had circulated among scientists, professors, engineers and others to determine what and where the silver ball came from It was x-rayed, cut with a diamond saw and many different ways were used to discover what it was and what was the material. They surmised it came from the 'sky' somehow. I was asked to hold the silver ball to see if I could get an impression what this unusual silver ball was. As I held the silver ball, I went into a deep trance state and gave them a complex formula, which they studied. However, I was never informed if they discovered what the unusual silver ball was.

Rehel and the silver ball

Changing Times

Our spiritual group was strong and powerful, and we created a strong bond between us. We met twice a week for four and a half years. Then everything was going to change from the solid spiritual routine we had to a much different life for each of us. I started having 'premonition dreams' of what was going to happen to everyone.

I was the western director for a manufacturing company in Las Vegas. It was very lucrative and didn't expect any changes or upsets in the company. One particular dream informed me that I would not be working for the company much longer, I would no longer have a secretary, I would be given six weeks of severance pay, and there would be a time I would not work. The dream was concise and to the point.

Shortly after the premonition dream, I was out of a job, given six weeks of severance pay, and no longer had a secretary. The headquarters in Connecticut decided they would concentrate the business on the East coast and no longer be in Las Vegas.

Now, what was I going to do? I decided to devote more time to my spiritual life.

Shirley MacLaine just released her new book 'Dancing in the Light'. She told her story of going to New Mexico and having an experience regarding her 'past lives'. Because of her book, the place she visited was referred to as 'The Light Institute'. It was so interesting I wanted the same or similar experience.

I called for an appointment and was informed they were booked up for at least six months because of the huge interest the book had created. I asked them to call me if they had a cancellation. A few hours later I received a call asking if I could be there the next day at 1:30 PM. Instantly I said "Yes" without knowing if I could get a flight to Albuquerque. I would rent a car to drive the rest of the way. Everything was falling into place. I had never been to Albuquerque or the small town I was to drive to and I didn't have a wrist watch to tell me what time it was. I trusted the universe to get me there. I arrived ten minutes before my sessions were to begin. This 'spiritual experience' is one that I cannot describe, and was not like anything I had experienced before or since. New Mexico has a high energy and felt my new experience would further me on my path to enlightenment.

The sessions were 'past life recall' treatments where acupuncture needles were placed in different meridians to stimulate the cellular memories of past lifetimes held in the body.

It began by undressing completely, lying down on a massage table and covered with a light blanket. The lady performing this session meditated, said a prayer, and then put the acupuncture needles in different meridians to stimulate the cell memories in my body. She said that whatever came into my mind, just to let it happen, relax and pictures of different time periods would appear. When I first saw a picture, I thought I was making it up. I questioned how real it was, but the pictures were always specific.

In one of the sessions, I was being shown (in my mind) a man and woman on a planet that had been destroyed. They were near death and eating the dry, gray twigs upon the blackened ground to stay alive. A sound came that made them look up. What was it? They described a 'thing from the sky' which sat down on the ground and a platform protruded from the *thing*. They managed to crawl up the ramp into the *thing*. They sat on a cushion/pillow like floor and waited. A voice came and announced that he was the Commander of the *thing*. A green and blue gel substance appeared before them and were told (in their minds) to consume the gel, but the green gel was for the woman and the blue gel was for the man. This would help nourish them. Soon the 'thing' took off into the sky and they rested well. Before long the 'thing' sat down on the ground again, the platform protruded out so they could leave. As the woman began to leave, she looked at her body and it was changing into a healthy, tall, beautiful blonde, about thirty years old, dressed in a bright colored skirt and white peasant blouse with ribbons. She looked at her companion and noticed he was changing into a healthy, strong, man of about thirty also, and dressed in brown pants with large suspenders and a white shirt. It was taking him longer to change than she did. She wondered why. Instantly, she was told (in her mind) that it took him longer to change as he was older than she. The couple started to leave the 'thing' down the ramp to a path. On the right side of the path were the most magnificent mountains you could imagine, and on the left side of the path were palm trees, jungles and beautiful flowers. In my mind I thought it quite unusual, as I didn't know if there is such a place on earth that has the Andes Mountains and tropical jungles together in the same area. As the woman was leaving, she was told (in her mind) that they were to go into the mountain village church. The people would be put in a 'mind state' and the villagers would not question who they were or why they were there. After church they were to get into a cart pulled by oxen and go to their home. Their home was a comfortable wood cabin with an earth and grass roof. A plume of smoke billowed from the chimney. She then wondered why they were there and what were they to do. Instantly, she was told again in her mind that they had agreed to stay on the planet that had been destroyed so others could leave, and this was their reward. She was told they were in the village to help maintain, keep and teach the customs of the village people, and they were not to go into the valley for many years.

I felt this vision was quite significant and why was I shown it? It was obviously a story of long ago, because in today's language the 'thing' is called a 'space craft' and 'in the mind' means 'mental telepathy'. Then incredibly I was told the man and woman were in another life-time, and the couple was my third husband and me. I guess we had to finish something together in this life-time.

Each life-time we have is meant to clear the Soul's conflict. What I learned from this type of regression was to clear unresolved memories in order to go to a higher enlightenment for each lifetime we have.

Two weeks after leaving New Mexico I attended a UFO conference in Phoenix, Arizona. What I call the 'big shots' in the UFO community were there, Stanton Freidman, Brad Steiger, Dan Fry and more. When we had our first break everyone went outside by the swimming pool where tables had been set up to sell books, paintings, literature, gifts and a variety of UFO materials. As I walked around the swimming pool I spotted a huge painting and I couldn't believe what I was seeing. It was exactly like the vision I had received during my stay in New Mexico with the magnificent mountains on the right and the tropical jungles on the left. I looked for the artist's name and on the lower right-hand corner it said "psychic artist unknown." This is not a 'coincidence' and there are no accidents! What was the spirit world trying to tell me? I know experience is 'knowledge' and each experience moved me further on my spiritual journey.

****

I stopped traveling and attempted to find work, but was always turned down for one reason or another. I recalled being told I would be out of work for a while but for how long?

Finally, the voice within returned and said, "You are going to be moving north-northwest." Oh boy, did I want to argue with that one. I didn't want to live anywhere it snowed. And, that was all that was said.

One day Dean told me he would be moving to Reno. I was surprised and it was probably Dean moving north-northwest, not me.

Not long after that the voice within said, "You will be getting a job, you will move after January 18th to Reno, and you will live there just *shy of two years,* then you will move south-southwest." Oh no, not me, I did not want to live in snow and south-southwest meant Los Angeles and LA is not one of my favorite places.

Very soon I was presented with a new job in Reno. I would teach 'crime prevention' classes while living there.

The universe has a great way of turning your life around. The last year I lived in Las Vegas my home had been burglarized thirteen times. It was very scary, stressful and turbulent. It became so serious the police had me install bars on the windows, install an alarm system, and buy a short-barreled shot gun. I also had a bodyguard. It did not keep the perpetrators out. The police informed me if I moved, it would still happen as they felt the perpetrator or perpetrators were after me and not what was in my home to steal. So, who else would be well qualified to teach 'crime prevention'? Plus, my first husband was a police officer, and felt I had some knowledge in that area. I realized teaching 'crime prevention' was being of service to others and was relieved to start a new chapter in my life.

Lotto Ticket

Shortly after moving to Reno on a very boring Saturday, my mind was chattering and wondering what I should do for the day, when the silent *voice, thought* and a moving *picture* strongly presented itself into my head.

I was being *told* and *shown* to go to the nearest 7-11 Store, buy snacks and drive to Truckee, California. In Truckee I was to go to a 'particular' 7-11 Store and purchase a lotto ticket with the numbers being presented to me … in my head.

I tried to dismiss this very powerful instruction, but it repeated three more times so strong I finally relented.

I drove to the nearest 7-11 Store, bought snack and was on my way to Truckee. Again, the vision appeared in my head when loudly the voice shouted, "Take this exit!" And, my ego self said, "No, I'll take the next exit."

As I took the next exit and came to a stop sign, the vision of the 7-11 Store where I was to purchase the lotto ticket was to my right a few blocks away. Again, my 'free will' or stubbornness kicked in, so I turned left and drove to Squaw Valley instead of doing as spirit had instructed. I thought there would be another 7-11 Store where I would purchase the lotto ticket. As soon as I drove into Squaw Valley to my right was another 7-11 Store. I went immediately to get a ticket and marked the numbers spirit instructed me to play.

The lotto drawing was very large and many people were standing in line to purchase tickets. When I reached the clerk to purchase my lotto ticket, the machine would not take the ticket. The clerk tried several times, but it still would not take my ticket. Several people kept saying, "She has the winning ticket." The clerk commented it was just my ticket and had me rewrite the ticket five different times. The customers began to argue with the clerk saying, "The machine takes everyone's ticket, it just isn't taking hers!"

It became quite a spectacle and at the last resort, the clerk finally called for the manager. The manager opened the lotto machine and as she did the large containers of jerky and sausage that were in front of the machine fell down and hit the top of my foot. Now, I was injured and the next half hour was spent filling out an accident report. I did not purchase my lotto ticket!

Oh, I was in pain and all I could think about was getting into the car and driving a couple blocks to the

Truckee River and put my ever so swelling foot into the ice-cold water.

As I sat on the river bank, I did my best to talk to spirit. But, nothing! I kept open and waited and still no answer. It was getting late so I drove back down the mountain and continued asking spirit, "What do you want me to do?" I did not do as instructed, so why did I expect an answer? Then, spirit put me to a test.

Driving the winding road down the mountain back to Reno, I heard, "Stop at McDonald's." I began to argue but quickly decided to pay attention. Spirit said, "Go to the restroom." So, I went directly to the restroom. As I started to leave, I heard, "Buy a hamburger." I started to argue again saying, "I don't eat McDonald's hamburgers." Just stop it I thought!

At that point I thought it was better do as I was being told. I bought a hamburger, got into my car and heard nothing more from spirit. I decided to drive to the first 7-11 Store that was shown in my vision and there I would purchase the lotto ticket.

As I drove into the parking lot I was in such pain with my injured foot, I sat there and sat there and decided I was in too much pain to walk into the store. I put the car in gear and drove back to Reno.

When I arrived home my only thought was to go upstairs to bed, prop up my foot and watch TV. Later the news would be coming on and I wanted to listen for the winning lotto numbers. The moment arrived and the numbers I was to play WERE the WINNING numbers, and I had not played my ticket!!! NO, no, no!!

What a great lesson. This can happen when you don't listen to what spirit is guiding and instructing you to do, especially when it is for your benefit. I can only imagine how my life might have turned out had I listened to this very important message. What did spirit want me to accomplish with that amount of money? Millions!!

Spirit followed with this message, "You will not have this opportunity again."

New Career

The course of events was about to take another turn in my life once again.

A production company from Hollywood came to Reno to film the movie Kill Me Again and asked if I could help them. Of course! This would be so exciting. After several weeks, they were leaving for Las Vegas to finish filming and asked if I would go with them to work with the Producer. When they finished filming in Las Vegas they asked if I would move to Los Angeles and work at their studio, but I refused as I still had my teaching job.

My friend Lincoln had already gone to LA to see if he could work in the movie industry.

Not long after that, my teaching job came to an end and wondered what was next for me. I asked the 'spirit world' what I should do. Yes, I was to move *south-southwest* to Los Angeles, just like the voice within told me before I moved to Reno. And, it was just *'shy of the two years'* the spirit had informed me long ago.

As I was moving into my new apartment in Burbank, I heard, "Don't unpack, you are not staying long." Why was all of this happening?

I worked three months for a top producer in the movie industry when I had an *'urging'*, not a *thought* or *voice* that I was to move to Palm Desert, California. I had no idea why Palm Desert. But the *urging* made it very clear I was to move, so I moved to Palm Desert.

I found a job at one of the beautiful country clubs, yet the salary was so low I wondered if I could pay my bills and wished I could get at least $200 more a month. I was not to start work for two weeks and went to Las Vegas for a visit. Upon returning to Palm Desert there was a message on my recorder, "Please call right away." Fear struck me, *what if* they don't want me, *what if* their plans had changed? I bravely called and this is what was said, "Hi, I'm so glad you're back, can you start right away, and by the way we are going to start you at two hundred dollars more a month, is this okay with you?" Oh, the spirit world heard my plea!

A few months later I began to have such deep depressing emotions. What was it? The job was good, I had several new friends and was having fun so what was so disturbing? I saw no apparent reason to feel this way. I had leased an apartment for six months and was considering if I should extend the lease or find a different place. I became more depressed, agitated and couldn't make any rational decisions. I cried out, "Please, please what is wrong, I'm so unhappy, I don't know what to do."

I had to talk to someone. I called my friend Marlis to cry on her shoulder, and said my lease was up and didn't know if I should renew the lease or not. She mentioned the complex had several vacancies and not to worry. She could tell how distraught I was and suggested I go to an oasis not far from Palm Desert to meditate and clear my thoughts.

All the way to the oasis I was sobbing so hard I could barely see to drive. I found the oasis and was relieved that no one else was there. I just couldn't face people in my state of mind. I walked through the oasis until I came to a clearing where I could see the desert all around me and, then, I *heard,*

"Sit down." I obeyed the command. "Pick up a stick and in the sand make a calendar." A 'force' was moving my hand on the stick.

"On this date you will quit your job, on this date you will move out of your apartment." My thoughts were rattling in my head and I asked, "How can I do this, I need this job and have no one to help me move?"

"You will leave your job on this date, and someone will help you move. Put your things in storage."

The answers I received created more despair. I wasn't hearing anything more, but was *urged* to start walking again. I kept walking and crying until I came to a small stream and sat down on the bank with my feet in the cool water. Feet in the water, eyes shut and doing my best to calm down, I opened my eyes and at the top of one of the desert hills was a huge white cross. Oh, this took my breath away. Surely this was another sign. As I continued to sit, I had more *thoughts* and *visions*.

"Leave at 8:00AM, go down this highway (seeing everything in my mind) go to this town. You are to go to Sedona, Arizona, stay at the Sky Ranch Lodge. Before you get there, you will be given a sign." That ended the communication.

When I arrived home, I turned on the answer machine; the apartment manager informed me I had to move out as my apartment had been rented to someone else. I instantly called Marlis crying, "What am I going to do, they rented my apartment."

She laughed at me, "You wanted an answer how clear do you want it? It's obvious you are not to renew your lease." I didn't tell her about the messages I had received while at the oasis, she would surely think I had finally gone off the deep end.

As instructed, a couple of days later I resigned from my job and told them I would be moving. One of the men at the resort overheard my conversation, and offered boxes and two men to help me move from my apartment just like I had been *told*. These two men didn't speak English, moved me in a flash and Marlis invited me to stay the night. That was the last home of any kind I had for many years. (1990 until 2000)

Early the next morning before getting on the road I stopped for gas. The service attendant was too busy to take my money so I went inside to buy snacks and a map to make sure there was a highway and town I had been shown in my vision. I didn't want to get lost in the middle of nowhere. I came out of the store to get in my car and had accidently locked the doors with the keys inside. I asked the attendant to help me but every time he tried to help another car drove up for service. This happened several times. I had wasted a lot of time. Both of us tried all four doors and when the attendant was not busy, he did the strangest thing. He put his face on the driver's door, looked over to the passenger side and in his broken English said, "Lady that door not locked."

I said, "It has to be, both of us have tried to open all of the doors." He repeated, "No, lady, that door not locked" and walked around and opened the passenger door. I looked at my watch. It was NOW just 8:00 AM. I *was not to leave before 8:00 AM...* as spirit had advised.

****

Ready for my new experience I started down the highway on my way to Sedona, Arizona. After a few hours I turned on the new highway that was in my vision, and before long I arrived in the town seen in the vision, it was Prescott, Arizona. Leaving Prescott, soon I was in a very flat area, no trees, homes, just wide-open space when suddenly I *heard,* "Look for me in the birds," and almost instantly, flying directly at my windshield came an owl and thought it was going to hit the windshield. I knew this was 'the' sign from the unseen forces.

I arrived in Sedona late afternoon but was unable to find the Sky Ranch Lodge. I stopped at a book store and asked for directions. A gentleman customer said he was staying there, but I needed to hurry as they were generally sold out. When I got to the Sky Ranch Lodge, I was informed there was only one room left. I knew I had to take it.

After checking in, *thoughts* were coming to me. I was to go to the 'airport vortex', lie down on the ground and meditate. Where was this vortex? The front desk clerk said I had just past it a few blocks from the lodge and gave me directions. I did as I was instructed by spirit and climbed the hill to the vortex.

While lying in the vortex, my body was tingling, feeling pressure and dizziness, but heard nothing and stayed as long as I thought was necessary. I walked down the hill and drove to a nearby restaurant to get a take- out order to eat back in my room. What a mistake! I had eaten a few bites when I became very ill. I couldn't eat or sleep. Then I recalled messages I had received long ago about entering a vortex. You are to bathe, not eat or drink for a couple of hours prior, and not to eat or drink for several hours after, and I had forgotten this very important message. I was miserable the next twenty-four hours.

I apologized to spirit for not remembering, but no matter what I said, or asked, I wasn't receiving any messages.

The next morning, I thought - I saw the town, I saw the owl, I reached my destination and meditated in the vortex, now what am I to do? Not hearing anything, I took a walk through the pine and cedar trees to enjoy the beautiful country of Sedona. Still no message, I checked out of the Lodge, drove around Sedona feeling pretty confused, and decided to get my car washed. As I drove to get the car washed, I *heard,* "Don't wash your car, it will just get dirty." Then *urged* to drive north which would take me to Flagstaff, Arizona. My journey began again!

Arriving in Flagstaff I was 'directed' to stop at a restaurant, continue driving to Page, Arizona where there would be a 'production' company. I paid attention and did as I was instructed to do, but I couldn't help feeling I was being controlled by some force. This felt like insanity, but I didn't know what else to do.

When I arrived in Page, Arizona I automatically drove to the 'production' company that was filming the movie 'Beastmaster'. How did I know exactly where to go? I knew an unseen force was guiding me all the way.

I went into the production office and asked where the filming location was and perhaps get a job with them as I needed money. They were filming approximately twenty-five miles out in the desert and was given directions how to get there. I wasn't sure I was on the right dirt road and the dirt road was a good reason not to have the car washed, as I had been told that morning.

Before long I saw in the distance a vehicle coming toward me leaving a big dust trail. I would stop the vehicle and ask if they knew where the production company was filming in case I was lost. The vehicle was a white van coming to a stop. I couldn't believe my eyes, it was my dear friend Lincoln driving the van and all he said was, "I knew you'd be here." Can you just imagine? I knew this would be important on my spiritual journey.

I started working a few days later in the production office. A local American Indian lady came in and seemed to pay special attention to me, but said nothing. I like the American Indian people and my first crush was on a young Indian boy when we lived on the ranch in Nevada.

One night sitting in my motel room there was a knock on the door. Standing there were three Indians, one male and two females. They announced they had a message for me however, the negativity in the motel was too strong and would it be possible to sit in the motor home parked outside. (Lincoln's motor home)

As we settled in, the male Indian said they were to cleanse and pray for me. He lit a dried clump of sagebrush, waved it around and chanted in his native language. The two females rubbed articles they had brought with them. This ceremony took several minutes before it was concluded. They presented me with some kind of rock and said I was to go on this 'journey or trek'. I was to listen to the spirits for guidance, what to do, where to go and they would be my guardians and protectors so no harm would come to me. They informed me I would be traveling, spend a great deal of time in Los Angeles, and work for the movie industry, and I would not have a home of my own for ten years. Working in the movie industry was going to be my new career!

I asked the male Indian why the movie industry as it is a very negative and difficult business. The wise Indian informed me that my purpose was to simply *'touch lives'* no matter where I went or who I met. My energy would touch their lives even if I did not speak or get acquainted with people. Then the three left and I never saw or heard from them again.

I do believe they were my protectors as I was in some very serious and unsafe conditions such as being shot at on the freeway while the guy next to my car was killed, or when I was in the middle of the chaos in Watts, California and so much more.

The Indians told me I would be on a ten year 'trek' and recalled spirit also telling me I would be on a ten year spiritual journey. Oh boy, the next ten years were unusual and extremely challenging.

During my stay in Page, Arizona, I began *hearing, seeing and feeling* what I was being directed to do. I was not to go back to Los Angles yet, but was to travel certain highways, to visit places where I lived as a child. After visiting these places, I was to stay with my father and review my life up to that point. During each visit, place or event, I would receive the next instructions. This was fascinating but I felt I must be losing my mind. Who in the world would live this way?

I followed *most* of the instructions and when I didn't it was as if someone smacked me good. There was always a price to pay in one form or another, which made it more challenging.

Staying with my father and not working, money was becoming a big concern. I needed a job and my funds were very low when another amazing scenario began.

My funds had depleted to sixteen hundred dollars when I got a call to work for another production company filming a TV movie in Los Angeles. The job would last twenty-five days and the money would sustain me so I could start back on my journey. I didn't realize until later working in the movie industry was all part of the journey.

Every time my funds were down to sixteen hundred dollars, I got another call for work with another production company, and this scenario continued for several years, always down to the last sixteen hundred dollars. I always had enough money to pay for necessities, but I wanted more. Why couldn't I have more? I had so many questions. I guess my 'life blueprint' had more for me to learn.

Letting Go

This pattern of life continued for another few years and I was getting very disenchanted with everything. The majority of time was spent with my friend Lincoln as we generally worked on the same movie. Every chance we got we went to Las Vegas to be with our spiritual group. However, all had changed since Lincoln and I left, Dean moved to Reno, Cecilia to Kansas, but Tom, Larry and Delores were still there. I felt each time I came back it was my only connection to reality and my spirituality.

As time went on, I was depressed and felt the challenges were too much. I doubted all that had happened in the past, felt nothing was real and I just didn't want to continue on this journey any longer. It was time I told the 'spirit world' enough is enough and to leave me alone. I wanted to be normal, live and act normal like everyone else. I did exactly what Tom told me. "The spirit world will leave you alone if you tell them." So, I totally dismissed the spiritual world. I wanted nothing to do with the kind of life I had been living. The spirit world promptly obeyed my command, and there was no voice within, messages, urges, premonitions, or visions. I was now alone in my new reality.

For another several years I lived what I call a 'normal' life, working in the movie industry, spending time with my non-spiritual friends, stayed with my father and son when I was not working and had more peace of mind than I had in a long time. Also, met a wonderful man and planned to be married. However, that was short lived. We were not compatible enough to have a good marriage. Even though I told my spirit guides to leave me alone, I felt they helped or nudged me to make the right decision not to marry this man.

I have always said your life path is like going from A to Z. We start a 'A' follow the path for a while, then we get to 'D' and take a detour (our choice) and continue on our detour until it's no longer in our best interest. Then the universe smacks you in some way and brings you back on course. You start again at E and continue on the path until you decide to take another detour, perhaps at K until it is no longer beneficial for you and then the universe brings you back on course. This continues your entire life until you reach 'Z'. All the detours you take are all the 'lessons' or 'challenges' you needed to experience for your spirit and soul growth while here on earth. I think I took way too many detours!

As time passed, life was not for the better. I was not content and life became a struggle. Depression set in, but I concentrated on work and making money so I could leave one day. I had no idea what would be in my future.

Still working in the movie industry, I was called to work on the movie 'Starship Troopers', which would last several months. We traveled to Wyoming and South Dakota to film and I had the most fun I had in a long time. As soon as that movie ended, I started on the movie 'Air Force One' back in Los Angles which would also be for several months. Right away problems started and it became the show from 'hell', but I didn't care, I was there to make enough money to leave. I was so focused on making money I didn't pay attention to the problems that would soon affect me greatly.

Gossip started about me and other females. I was pulled into a sexual harassment complaint with the Teamsters Union. I was being threatened by a 'certain' group, 'black balled' in the business and I feared for my life. Who I thought were my friends were no longer my friends! I tried the best I could to stay focused on making money and convincing myself it would be over in a few short months. I did take steps with the 'leader' of the group that had threatened me. I presented my case and left my fate in his hands, but was still very afraid.

A week went by when he approached me, gave me a signal and I knew I had nothing to fear from then on.

I didn't realize how much the stress was taking on my body. My health was failing, developed diverticulitis in the critical stages, and spent four days in the hospital with extreme infection. The doctors wanted to operate, but I just wouldn't take time off work.

When the movie was completed a few weeks later, I agreed to have the colon surgery. I was admitted into the Motion Picture Hospital in Calabasas, California. I developed serious problems as the epidural was left in my spine for three days after the surgery. I was being paralyzed from the waist down.

I had pushed my dear friend Lincoln out of my life, he had left the movie industry and I needed help. As a good friend does, he was right there by my side. The doctors were worried and didn't know how long it would take before I would regain the use of the lower part of my body. The pain was unbearable.

One night I was very frightened and felt I was going to die. I had never been afraid to die before, but this time I was terrified. I asked the nurse to call the Chaplain. I wanted his prayers and wasn't ready to go to the other side yet. The Chaplain couldn't be reached, so the nurse came into my room, knelt on the floor beside my bed and prayed the 23rd Psalm. The prayer comforted me and released me from the terror, but still very ill. Several days later feeling somewhat better, I was released from the hospital and returned to the hotel I had been staying at during filming of the movie. Lincoln had returned to his home in Washington and I would spend another five months, alone at that hotel, and slowly regained use of my legs, yet still was not well.

Not fully recuperated from the surgery, my body in a sensitive state, I suffered from food poisoning three different times. My father passed away, and that shook my world to the core. I felt totally alone for the first time in my life. The day after the funeral in Salt Lake City, I was called to work on the movie Parent Trap being filmed in Napa Valley, California, and knowing I was not well enough to work, I agreed to work anyway.

Once the movie was completed, I decided to visit my son and his family in Truckee, California. My daughter-in-law and I took a walk in the beautiful Sierra Mountains and within minutes of returning home I experienced extreme flu like symptoms with high fevers that lasted two weeks. I took loads of antibiotics and felt close to death once again.

When I regained some strength, my son and Dean drove me back to Los Angeles to see my personal doctors. I was immediately put in the hospital and then back in the same hotel fighting to get well. Shortly after settling into the hotel, I had three kidney surgeries and spent another five months going from the hotel into the hospital trying to get well. My only contacts were occasional long distance phone calls with friends or my son. And, now my life was going to take another turn in the road. Maybe I had been on this detour long enough!

As the months went by, I finally had a couple more doctor appointments before I would be released to go back to work. I needed to make up my mind what I should do and where I should go as I could not endure staying in that hotel any longer.

During those five months I had a hard time remembering my name. Was it because of the surgery, medication or stress? Sometimes my name would come back to me, but most of the time, it did not.

Many years ago, I was interested in Ann Ree Colton, known as a 'modern day prophet'. She had written many books and started the Ann Ree Colton Foundation in California. I had no idea where her Foundation was located.

On one particular day as I left the doctor's office for the last time, driving the freeway back to the hotel, still wondering what I should do with my life, and after so many years of not having the *voice within* I heard, "Go to the Ann Ree Colton Foundation."

Surprised to hear the *voice within* again, I said, "I don't know where the Foundation is," with intentions to shrug it off. And, immediately, I heard, "What else do you have to do?"

It was said in such a commanding, yet loving tone, I didn't argue. Back in the hotel, looked in the phone book, and much to my surprise, the Ann Ree Colton Foundation was six blocks away!

Immediately I drove to the Foundation and walked through the wonderful flower gardens and paths when I noticed that Ann Ree had passed away several years earlier and her ashes were placed by a beautiful statue. All the doors to the Foundation were locked, but when I tried to open another door a lady asked if I needed help. I commented I had read many of Ann Ree's books and was interested in the Foundation. She mentioned the Foundation was never open on a Friday, but she just *happened* to stop by ... coincidence? She invited me to their gathering that evening, which I gladly accepted.

I was greeted by the most loving people who seemed genuinely interested in me and was enjoying the spiritual connection. As I was sitting with an elderly lady, she said, "What is your name?" Oh dear, I could not remember my name! I attempted to tell her I was having difficulty remembering my name for some time and had no explanation for it. She promptly got up and left me sitting there. I thought I might have insulted her, but shortly after, a beautiful blonde lady came to greet me and said she had been told I was having trouble remembering my name. I repeated the story to her, she seemed interested but the subject went no further.

The next week I joined more of the gatherings. During the last event, the same beautiful blonde lady asked if I would like to attend their Sunday Service, which I accepted gladly. She then told me she had *'received'* a new name for me, and I would be presented with this new name at the Sunday service and would I accept it?

The service began and little did I know that the beautiful blonde lady was Shone Marie, who had replaced Ann Ree and Ann Ree's husband after their passing. The spiritual gifts had been passed on to Shone Marie. The members conducting the ceremony were all dressed in white robes, surrounded by an array of red roses. After delivering the Sunday message, I was called forward to kneel in front of the members conducting the service. I was anointed with fresh rose water, given bread and wine, and the most beautiful prayers spoken over me. I was then given the name 'Rehel' which means 'an angel who battles the enemies of spirit and religion.' I was told the name would change the energy for me and my life would change rapidly should I choose to use this name. I was told by members of the congregation how unusual it was for anyone to be given a name in such a short time and most members didn't receive a name for years, if ever. How blessed I felt, however, I decided not to use the new name Rehel. Not yet anyway.

The Return

Finally, my body was getting better and I wanted to go back to work. Little did I know the sexual harassment complaint had not gone away, and no one wanted anything to do with me, but I no longer had to fear for my life! What was I do, I just couldn't stay in that hotel any longer so I called Larry and asked if I could stay with him for a while.

Deep inside I started having *urges* like I once had. One of the *urges* felt like I was to move to Hawaii or Arizona. I loved those two places, yet it seemed impossible for me to go there, so I discounted the feelings.

Arriving in Las Vegas at Larry's home I was excited to be around a friend. By the second day I was in deep despair. Larry was treating me like he had never treated me before. He was rude, angry, impatient, and had such animosity toward me. I wondered why he had agreed to let me stay with him. I visited another friend, but her life was in shambles. What was I to do?

As luck would have it, or some 'divine' intervention, a friend from the Ann Ree Foundation called. She was going to Scottsdale, Arizona for the weekend and asked if I would like to meet her. Oh yes, I couldn't get out of Las Vegas fast enough.

A long time later, Larry and I had a conversation about how he treated me. He said he did not recall what happened and he would never treat me that way. Both of us believed it was 'divine' intervention that pushed me further on my life's journey.

I spent a nice weekend in Scottsdale and decided to stay after my friend left. I couldn't afford to stay in a motel very long as my funds were low not working. I looked for a corporate condo to rent for a month or two. It would give me enough time to figure out what I should do next.

The *universe* or *spirits* were working for me again, even though I wasn't aware of it at the time. The complex where I was to rent was closed on Sunday, but the agent made a special trip to rent it to me within twenty minutes. This is how the universe works! Helping me!

The energy, people and surroundings in Arizona were incredible. I felt very good, yet I got very depressed and felt so lonely again. I didn't have anyone to talk to and felt life was not worth living. I just wanted to die. I was giving up. I no longer wanted this struggle or the challenges anymore.

I called my friend Gary, a psychologist in LA, and cried my eyes out, clear to the depths of my soul. Whatever was said I didn't remember, but that night I searched my soul. My thoughts brought me back to the night in the hospital after my surgery when I almost died. My inner being kept telling me, "If you didn't die, then there is something you are meant to do. God wants you to do something." I kept hearing this statement in my head over and over. I meditated, which I hadn't done in a very long time. I heard nothing and decided to write a letter to the spirit world, hoping they would hear me. Before long I had a response, using automatic writing. The response started out with "Surprise, surprise, it's about time you contacted us," and I was able to receive messages from then on.

I knew my only way back to a peaceful life was to be with God and the spirit world. What a long detour I had taken. After being away from the spirit world it doesn't magically change. I still had many decisions to make and learn how to listen to the *voice within* once again.

First, I expressed my gratitude for everything I had been through. Second, I found a 'new age' type church where I could meet like-minded people. Next, I went to a person that does energy balancing using acupuncture, meditation and crystals to get my energy back on track. She told me in about ten days my life would change and people would respond to me differently. At that time, I decided to use my new name 'Rehel'. This was my return to the spirit world.

I met many wonderful people and it was over two months since I had arrived. I hadn't worked in a long time and needed money. The movie industry was getting busy and I decided to go back to LA to find work, but wondered how I would respond to the people that had given me so many problems. Could I take the stress if nothing had changed? I asked the spirit world to help and guide me. It also meant going back to LA I needed to use my old name DeAnne.

Right away the union called and I was to work as a 'day player' which means you work one day for a production, then one or two days at another production. Whatever work I could get, I would be most grateful. The union has thousands of members, and my chances of working with my half dozen enemies, as I called them, were slim, so I thought.

This is how the spirit world works. The first call to work was with one of those enemies. I prayed for as much help as I could get. The next morning stressed and dreaded going to work, the first person I saw was the enemy, walked up to me gave me a big hug and was glad to see me. I was stunned. Oh, thank you spirit world! The next day I was called on another job with another one of my enemies. What are the chances of that? Same story, stressed to the max and again when I arrived, the enemy gave me a big hug and was glad to see me! This same story repeated itself every day, with every enemy, until I could think of only one enemy left. What were the odds of any of this happening, but I was not about to doubt what the spirit world was trying to do – I was to make amends!

The final call came for work again, and this would be with the worst of my enemies. Even though everything had turned out great with the previous people and work, was I able to withstand this one? When I arrived on set, I saw this person coming towards me and I instantly looked down hoping I would be left alone. Oh no, this person walked right up to me shouting, "It's good to see you, how are you" and gave me a big hug. We worked together for the next three weeks, and after that I was called with leads for constant work. I worked for about six more months and finally decided to retire and make a new life in Arizona. I had been in the movie industry fifteen years and that was enough!

I realized the lady that did the energy work, said "People will treat you differently." Yes, not just that, but I believe it was *my return* to the *spirit world*. And, if Larry had not pushed me away would I have gone to Arizona? That is where spirit wanted me to be to continue my spiritual journey.

The Journey Continues

Lincoln also left the movie industry and moved back to his home town, but I still did not have a place to call my own. I'd been fortunate enough to stay with family and friends for short periods of time.

Excited to be back to Arizona, I rented the same corporate condo I had rented before. I met many people and had a group of new friends. I felt this was my new home, yet there was something still missing or undone in my life. What was it? Then the manager of the condo said I had to move as my condo had been rented to someone else for the summer. Where was I to go? Luckily my friend George, from church, said I could stay with him as long as I needed. I accepted his invitation and was thankful for a place to live.

I had been at George's a couple of weeks when driving down the freeway (seems to be where I get some messages) when I heard with urgency, "You must meet Betty Colburn." And, the message kept repeating.

I was confused. Bettye Colburn had become a friend to Lincoln who now lived in Spokane, Washington. He told me what a beautiful, spiritual, and knowledgeable person she was. Why was I being told to meet her? I learned from past experiences if I waited three days either the circumstances would change or there would be a definite command. The next three days the *voice within* did not leave me alone. It spoke with more urgency. "You must meet Bettye Colburn before February 15th." This must be important! I called Lincoln and arranged to meet Bettye Colburn.

I arrived in Spokane on February 14th, Lincoln picked me up at the airport and we drove directly to Bettye's home. When she opened the door, we got big hugs and I noticed what a sweet person she was. There were so many material objects in her house we had alike, which I pointed out to her. She simply said, "We must have a lot in common, and we must have been sisters in another lifetime."

Bettye had a very powerful energy, and changed many lives just being in her presence. At one time she worked for the governor of Texas, gave readings to the astronauts, wrote books, an astrologer, held classes and lectured on spirituality. And, because of her, I knew my life was going to make another change.

She invited friends from Idaho and Montana, but I would have three days with Bettye before they arrived. I learned she had a way of allowing the spirit world to do its work for you, and not to influence you or the 'process' that is to take place.

What I didn't know at the time, I was sent to Bettye because she assists persons going through a new **'*Soul Transference*'**. In the Chapter – Walk-ins, I explained the two types of Walk-ins, and now, I was going to go through a **new** '*Soul Transference*' a **Walk-In** of the **'Second Kind!**

One night Bettye, Lincoln, some of her friends and I were talking about the new astrology, blood lines, books and the new 'Gaia' chart (which means God's Angels in Action). I was standing, looking down over the charts while Bettye explained the differences of the Gaia chart and an astrology chart. All of a sudden, it felt like something hit me on the side of my head. I saw black and red then feel into a chair.

At the moment I had no recall of what was transpiring, but Bettye told me I was giving the three of them instructions what to do for me and the type of care I needed. When I became conscious, I felt terrible, also felt I was going to die and couldn't stop it. I felt I was fighting to stay alive for the next hour or so. And, Bettye said nothing about what was transpiring.

I asked Lincoln to leave and take me to his place. I put the car seat back, started praying and doing some of the rituals I did many years ago when I felt some negative entity or energy had intruded into me or my space. Nothing worked and I became more disoriented and confused. As we drove down the winding mountain road two large beautiful white wolves crossed in front of us. I knew seeing the two white wolves was a very significant sign connected to the spirit world. My body was weak and rubbery and I had no control. This was not like any near death or dying feeling I ever encountered before.

When we arrived at Lincoln's home I immediately got into bed. Then I caught myself saying and doing the strangest things. I thought the bed was very strange as if I had never been in it before. Lincoln came into the doorway and asked if I needed anything, before he retired and was I alright?

I rose up, put my hands together like a prayer and said, "Thank you for allowing me to be in your home." Now, this was quite ridiculous as we had known each other over seventeen years and been roommates many times. Why was I so formal? Then fell asleep as a 'stranger' in Lincoln's home.

The next morning, I looked in the mirror and was totally shocked. I called Lincoln and asked him to look at me and tell me if I looked different. He said I looked different, especially my eyes. This day my eyes had changed from being wide apart and a dark hazel brown in color to being closer together and a light hazel green color, and my eye sight was somewhat distorted. What had happened?

We drove to Bettye's right away and perhaps she could explain what happened to me the night before, for I surely had no explanation. I explained all of the 'unusual' feelings, how I was talking differently, how there was a change in my appearance, especially my eyes. And, all Bettye did was smile and said, "That's wonderful." I knew she knew what happened, why wouldn't she confide in me?

I accepted her silence and spent days with her and her friends in 'spirit world' conversations. During one of these very intense conversations and without warning, I began to *speak* for the universal spirits. I had not used my medium gifts to channel for many years, and wasn't sure I would ever do it again. This time I was not in a trance and had full knowledge what was being said. I was very alert to each side of both worlds; our world and the universal world simultaneously. I was operating in a 'duality' which I had never experienced before. I could interact in those conversations whenever I needed to clarify or answer questions someone might have regarding the channeled information.

In one of our sessions, I could see the universe, different planets and stars, dark and light. I could see different 'beings' and what they were doing. I was shown the 'Pearly Gates' which I laughed and said, "I thought that was just a story in the Bible or some religious symbol." I was shown different parts of heaven on the other side of the Pearly Gates and it was so beautiful. I was shown where you could see and talk with Jesus. I was shown where 'God' reigns, but you are not allowed there until 'later' and I didn't understand what 'later' meant and didn't ask. Then to my amazement, I was taken back out into space, where the person known as 'DeAnne' was presently working on a planet and completing part of her journey. She appeared very happy and relieved she was not in body or on earth any longer. It was then I realized why I had come to see Bettye.

Soul Transference

In a previous chapter 'DeAnne' became a Walk-In of the **first kind.** She lived her life as herself and was 'integrated with another soul' in order to 'help' her complete her mission on earth. The 'physical body' always resembled the original body of DeAnne. As she continued to live her life of challenges, the 'integrated soul' was more prevalent after twenty years. This is when DeAnne was given the name 'Rehel'. The new name helped her begin to release the energy or higher self of DeAnne and to prepare for another transition which would take place with this same physical body. And, that is why I was directed to Bettye Colburn, to use her expertise for a new 'Soul Transition'. This means releasing the first Walk-In to Walk-out and the new 'Soul' to **Walk-in**. That is why it's called a **Walk-in of the second kind.**

When DeAnne/Rehel encountered the 'Gaia' chart at Bettye's home and was made unconscious, the new 'Soul Transference' (of the second kind) began to take effect. That is what brought the confusion, the feelings of death and the noticeable physical changes. Bettye was not allowed to explain at the time what was going on, but in approximately two weeks she could say what I had actually experienced.

We continued our spiritual conversations, and in one of our sessions, we were told that 'DeAnne' had finally made the complete transition and we were to honor her, love her, and wish her the best. We were told not to mourn for her, even though the group cried many tears for losing the one they knew as 'DeAnne/Rehel'. It was as if we had a funeral for her. Also, at the time, I, Rehel now being a new Soul was instructed to use the name Joyele for a short time as Joyele would bring a more feminine energy to the new soul of Rehel, and the name Rehel had more of a masculine energy that needed to be balanced. Once the balance was attained, I was to continue using the name Rehel for the rest of time.

The following is a small part of the channeling session where we learned of the 'soul transition' of DeAnne to Rehel. This was channeled from 'Force' through Rehel. People from the group asked questions and *Force* gave these answers.

~ ~ ~ ~ ~

Lynn: What more can you tell us of yourself or selves?

Clarity, we, us, have not been, will not be, and am not, will not pertain to any individual, any being, any

105

spirit, any guide, any guardian, any Gods, no supreme being, for we are in relation to a 'Force' ONLY! Forces must contact individuals when specifically asked by those that have gone to greater and higher beings of work. Do you understand me? It is the 'Little One's' (DeAnne's) request that we come here today to encounter you for that individual purpose. Do you understand me? We are not of like mind of self; we are merely an entity of energy frequency coming to you through the request of the 'Little One', merely forcing you to understand the energy projection. There is quite a difference in the meaning of that 'form of prolification', linkages, connections that may interact with all things and all levels at different times. This being of our individualistic *form* is merely a *form* by request interacting with the 'Little One', so called *energy force* coming to you, to celebrate this day, this time, this place, in the now, in the here.

Bettye: Are there any specific things you were asked to share with us?

She (DeAnne) asked that we, as Force, have you understand that we come to celebrate with you to give you the feeling and words of condolence from the Little One as requested. For she was willing to take her place in another time and another spot, for her to exceed in her growing that she did here on earth with you. Much relevance was placed on the energy and asked to go

106

forth, for her knowledge was great then, but now must be attuned to a much higher vibration and to learn many things. We are simply and dutifully doing our best coming here for her sake and your sake, and to give you the warmth and appreciation of her for now. And, from time to time she will contact you in some way through others that you may contact or through the one now speaking (Rehel/Joyele). But we cannot and do not. We are normally the kind that come and relate any inferences or information into you, only upon request, by individuals such as the 'Little One' that departed, for they cannot in this time frame submit their energy back to you, so our force is being committed up to you to relate for her for now. And, then in the future when you have many interesting individuals come to you, which may be of Gods, of the space, of the spirit ones, or the being which protrude into minds or the thought form, which you call telepathy, will be given unto you. However, we are not those kinds and cannot be that kind.

Lynn: You are like an energetic greeting card.

Simply put. We do have much that we do. However, it is rarely on this plain and on occasion come to relate to someone or something on this planet. We are inter-connected with the space beings that fly around you daily that keep in contact with you. We are a 'force being' that they relate to, to help them with their ships, with their energy and we contact that inter-spatial travel as you talk about, for their guidance needs to be very strong and tough, and we help them. Do you understand? For we are like the magnet of energy that pushes forth through the eons or the words I'm seeking to find that you might understand. We are the *connection of all,* of all possible *prolificaries* as there could be.

Lynn: Have you always been that way or have you been in another form?

No, we were inter-connected some time ago. However, never had the form of bodies, or your form of species, or forms of atoms or particles.

Bettye: What is your connection with 'Joyele' that you are speaking through now?

We have none, merely a substitution for the ones that were here and merely an interjection for the one that asked us to pertain this message to you from the Little One. We cannot connect or interact directly with the one that took her place, (Joyele) which I assume now you are calling this one by that name?

Yes!

Lynn: At this particular moment is the Little One aware of your connection with us?

Much, much, knowing that you would be listening today, she was like a stepping stone going into orbit and could not continue her journey until she felt at peace with all of you here.

Bettye: We send her peace and love.

And she will be gratefully appreciating all that you give to her. There was a time of transition that she could relate to all of you and was willing to do that, however, by being projected into the future so quickly by your chart (Gaia) and what you were doing allowed that frequency to become so high it did project her faster than desired. Perhaps by the answer that I relate to you that when you do contact other individuals or beings from the 'Source' they can give you the answer about the chart and if you should continually use it in the future or not, however, we cannot do that.

Bettye: I understand. She had a contractual agreement that's why!

We all ask that you support *beings* that come around you for the *next decade* at least. We are about to suppress some of the energy coming to earth to see if we can help guide those individuals of tyrant to form a different type of energy that has become prevalent upon your planet. This planet is in quite disarray and those individuals coming to the 'beings of harassment' will be subdued some and if it takes our energy to interact, we are going to place ourselves with the Gods so they might have the forces to inter-connect with you and then to *help save all* if need be. We cannot interlock completely for our attunement would be too much of a chaotic force and could blow your universe into a totally different orbit than what is *schedule* to be.

Lynn: You mean like a conduit?

Not like your meaning of conduit. We are a force that is spinning out in space that is in direct contact with space ships, it is all a force of energy that allows ships to travel at tremendous speeds and forces to encounter universe after universe, or solar systems, and to move about in ways that you seem to have some knowledge of. We are as if there was a fuel or gas tank in an automobile, we are that form to the craft.

Betty: Is that similar to our understanding of the ether?

It is much more of a combination than that. There is no relevance to the force of what I'm speaking, it is so tremendous in relation to your thoughts, there would be no understanding and that's why we have chosen to use words 'we' and why we use the name of the 'Force'.

Lynn: Is it similar to our concept of the black holes?

110

NO.

Robin: Is it where we in 3rd dimension understanding free energy can be pulled from?

NO. What I'm attempting to do is relate to you that this is a force so strong that your concept of energy, feeling, forces could not be comprehended. It is suggested that perhaps I should use the word 'power planet'.

Bettye: Perhaps we could harness this energy. Does that permit us to contact you?

Again, I am not allowed to give you all of this information, but what I can do is relate this information to the proper 'sector' to relate this information. However, with the knowledge that I have, and I'm being allowed to give you is, that your harnessing of energy means that you can contact energy force fields of substantial energies, frequencies, relativity, electricity, all the known factors that you seem to be eloquently describing is that, it is a force out there of a conducting force. However, again, I must say *you do not contact this force,* which the words I am using now are, we as individuals meaning this is a force beyond any control that you could possibly contact at any time, for our main mission is merely to subside and give the currents of energy supposedly to the craft and the inter-spatial conductors.

Bettye: You mention the craft. Is the Little One on a craft now?

Not at this time. Upon repeating what I was saying, she has been taken to an area which was known to you in your communication yesterday, when you were talking about Nebulas, the Anunnaki Tribe, and the conducting areas thereby. However, to get to these individuals, she did take a part of a *skip* on a craft.

Bettye: She is being treated with courtesy and kindness and love?

Much was given her upon relation to your contact with her and upon arriving she was given much treatment of kindness, individually, personally and spiritually. All of the combinations were given her because the attunement that she had asked for and giving her what she had recommended for us to give you in return. Thank you from her for the blessings, help and understanding. Her tears come to you.

Lincoln: We all loved her, and we thank her for all the wonderful information she has given us. We miss her and she will not be forgotten.

Bettye: She was a great blessing in our life.

As she is able to proceed farther in what she has assumed to do in her contractual agreement, she is also

112

making an inter-connection with groups of individuals. As I repeat again, those spirits, those beings, those Gods, those space brothers, and any angel that come about her, will have the opportunity to relate aback to you some of the messages. And again, I repeat that right now, this time, this day, this space, she is not allowed to do that or the other forces that she contacts are also not allowed to come into this and by her requiring us, that is the only reason we have been allowed to come into this force field. What I am explaining to you is a force, only being requested are we allowed to do that, and as this one known as the Little One has asked by request to relate to you the pleasure, the hopes and the fear.

Bettye: We honor that we could be present and assist during the transition for both.

Your specific thoughts and individual hearts of assumption will go to her with our contact and bring it back to her for she will know you are in peace, love and attunement. And, be rich in your spirituality, and contact, and have faith, and no fear, and subject yourselves to the kindness of others, as you give love to those that you meet, and your attunement will rise upon request and you must not have any care or fear of the loss of the Little One because that information will be in touch with you at all times. It will take approximately fourteen days in your time before she will be able to get others to come and show you some kind of a substance,

113

or a contact, or a memory, or a thought, which pertains to her. There will be a way that she will absolutely let you know that she has all, feels all, and be with you, and especially in times of need, and with your understanding. You know that she will be operating subsequently on line 1, 2, and 3 thereby giving her much support in the other dimensions that she will be working on too. And, this will be in relation to God, and all higher beings and help, for much was done on this agreement between her and God, and those individuals between here and there. And please, if you would just be patient and give her those fourteen days of your time. The time is exceedingly moving and we must depart now, and we give blessings to each one of you in this room. Much health, wealth, prosperity, clear thinking, and abundance will come to all of you. Hearts-minds meld together. You are a glorious bunch of beings and hopefully if we are permitted have the privilege of contacting you again. And now, as it may sound somewhat corny in this individualistic state of mind, as they say "God be with you."

Everyone in the room …. "And so, with you!"

End of the channeling transmission

Bettye Colburn & Rehel

Again, I felt like the person going through the 'government witness protection program'. This time it was stronger than ever. I could grasp memories, like reading a book, but had no emotional attachment to the people or memories that I encountered in my head. Even my new friends in Arizona seemed like strangers to me, yet I was willing to begin a new life with the new soul that this body had now transformed into.

Once I returned to Scottsdale, I used the name Joyele and no one seemed to be concerned about the name change. Within six months I was spiritually told to return to the name Rehel. Today I am Rehel and most of my friends only know me as Rehel.

I saw Bettye a couple more times and I let go of most of my friends and family as I had changed. I felt no connection to any of them and I was starting a whole new life.

A Home at Last

I was retired from the movie industry and it was almost ten years since I had a home of my own or any semblance of a normal life. I wanted to buy a house, but I wasn't having any success and if it didn't work one way, I would try another way. I didn't have much money and didn't have a job which made it more difficult as my credit report looked pretty bleak. I was getting discouraged and the *voice within* was not cooperating. "Just tell me what to do" I shouted. Still no answers! At one point I gave up and let it go, not knowing what else to do.

My dear friend Millie from Utah invited me to take as trip to Alaska for two weeks. And, at that time I decided to leave Arizona and said goodbye to all of my friends and didn't believe I would be back. I said, "God, I leave this in your hands," and I would live in the present moment as I didn't have any idea where I would go after the Alaskan trip.

We stayed with Millie's friends seeing Alaska and in the evening hours we would be on the lake fishing as the summer days are very long. What a change from the lower 48 states! The second day after we arrived. I received a phone call from a housing development in

Arizona. They heard I wanted to buy a home and would I be interested in a co-op townhouse? It was two a story with two bedrooms, two bathrooms. It was available immediately, but I needed to sign the papers and express mail a check that day. I asked how much it cost and what if I didn't like it once I saw it? They stated I would get my money back, but it was important for the new buyers to qualify for their new home. I figured I had nothing to lose and thought this might be the only way I could buy a home. I faxed the contract and sent a check for $3,500 by Federal Express that day.

Thoughts of confusion rattled my mind. What did I do, buying something I never saw, and at such a low price, was it a drug house, did it have walls, was it trashed? What did I do this time!

Once I calmed down, I thought about being in Arizona again with friends and a place to call my own and got more excited about my new plan. I marked off the days on the calendar to see when the vacation was over and I would return to Arizona. When I looked at the calendar, the date was June 29, 2000, and **exactly 10 years to the day** the Indians said I would be on my Spiritual **Trek.** Oh, thank you Universe! Timing is everything and the universe gives it to you when it is the right time.

Returning to Scottsdale two weeks later, I was worried, yet excited about seeing the co-op home I had just purchased. I didn't know what to expect. I held my breath as I walked up to the door and was very surprised how cute and how well kept it was. I would only need to put my personal touches on it to make it the perfect home for me. Now, I did not feel so displaced in the world – finally!

A Companion

What a new and exciting step forward this was going to be. I started by fixing up my cute little home to make it as comfortable as possible. Next, I started working on my body to feel better after so many injuries and surgeries, and was taking some of those self-help classes. How wonderful it was to settle down after just a gypsy life style.

Ready for another challenge, I put the word out to all friends that I was looking for a 'man' in my life! Most said they wouldn't introduce me to anyone because they thought I would just leave town again, while some thought I was joking as they couldn't imagine how I wanted to settle down after the life I had been living. But, once they understood I was serious, the word went out and I also prayed to the universe for my desire. This time I made sure I asked the universe for good qualities and character of a new man.

A couple of months went by when I had a 'feeling' I would meet someone from the state of Washington. This was a clue from the spirit world! Then I had a dream where I was at a baseball field. I saw a rather dirty, longhaired skinny man with a baseball cap on, not to my liking, then I was sitting with some friends on a patio when a 'black Cadillac convertible' drove by, and saw a tall man standing there, but his face could not be seen.

I called my friend Jeannie and told her the dream and she wasn't interested. But, three days later she called and said her boyfriend, Al, had found the man in my dream and he wanted to meet me and he has a dog. Do you like dogs and will you come to the ballgame on Sunday, she asked? How could I refuse?

A year earlier, Tom gave me a reading and told me I would meet a man with a dog.

Jeannie and I arrived at the ballpark where they were having a large baseball tournament being played on four fields with many teams and spectators. We walked by a row of bleachers, when a small dog was barking at us. I said to Jeannie, "That's his dog," and I looked out to one of the ball fields and said, "That's him on second base," and noticed the pitcher was the dirty, skinny, long haired man in my dream. Of course, Jeanine thought I was crazy.

Soon the man I picked out on the ball field walked up and Al introduced me to Jim with the small little dog that barked at us. The four of us went to a bagel shop and as we sat on the patio, a 'black' Cadillac convertible passed by, and I learned Jim was from the state of Washington. That was my dream confirmation!

The four of us separated as the men went back to the tournament and we went on our way.

As soon as I got home, I called Tom and told him I had met Jim. Tom in twenty years never said a good word about any man I met, but this time was quite different and immediately said, "He's the one."

Al had given Jim my phone number but he didn't call for over three weeks. He had been traveling for ball tournaments, would be back in two weeks and asked if I would go to dinner.

Jim arrived forty-five minutes late for our date and was limping. He had injured his Achilles heel playing softball. In the restaurant we sat in a quiet booth so we could talk and get acquainted. I decided to be honest about my life and my 'spiritual and psychic' abilities. This would either interest him or scare him away. ... And, that's how it began.

****

We had so much in common being on the road with no place to call home. He was an entertainer, owned a restaurant which he closed, and had a gypsy lifestyle traveling the country playing softball tournaments. But, now with a painful Achilles heel, he could no longer play softball. He was not happy staying with his friend and not sure what to do, so I introduced him to my friends, went to church and went to a Karaoke bar to sing since he was an entertainer.

I called Tom and repeated what Jim had told me. Tom immediately said to invite him to stay at my home, have him sleep on the couch and not to worry. What was he saying, I just met this man, how safe would it be, and I didn't let anyone stay at my home! Jim accepted gladly, moved in with a very few belongings and had my couch to sleep on.

We were together almost constantly and shared our life stories. I related all my stories of spiritualism, metaphysics, UFO's, heaven and earth, and taught him to read cards.

He said he prayed to God for a special person to come into his life, to stop traveling, and settle down. I am sure his 'divine intervention' was the painful Achilles heel to bring him to a stop, just like my injuries and surgeries that stopped me from working in the movie industry.

A few days of being together, the spirit world jumped in and surprised us both. As he lay on the couch, I went into trance, twisted my body into contortions and gave him a blessing and healing. I had not done that in a long time.

Later he did need surgery and the doctor said it would take a year before he was able to do much. However, six weeks after surgery the doctors were surprised how quickly he healed and released him so he could go with me to Costa Rica for twenty days. Yes, the spirit world had blessed him with a healing and we had become a couple to start a new journey together.

As time went on, still living in Scottsdale, we worked together in real estate, selling property in San Felipe on the Baja of Mexico. I thought it was the most awful place I had ever seen. One day touring all the properties, I stood on a barren lot, when I *felt strongly* that I was to buy the lot. Not in this horrible place! But spirit was *nudging* me to do just that, so before returning to Scottsdale, I purchased the lot. After returning to Scottsdale, *thoughts* came to me that I must build a house as soon as possible before the market changed. I did as spirit had instructed, and before long the house was under construction.

Jim got caught up in his work and he displayed a huge ego that I had not witnessed before. We were still working and building a house in Mexico and not having much fun at my expense. He was under such stress, which caused a heart attack and required heart surgery. Within thirty days he had gallbladder surgery. He bragged about his surgeries and required a lot of attention from everyone. The doctor told me it sometimes happens when a patient is close to death and how their personality changes after the type of surgeries he had gone through. His huge ego was not to my liking!

I was getting *urges* and *suggestions* from the spirit world for new opportunities and choices to improve our lives, both individually and as a couple, but Jim shrugged them off. One choice was to move to Panama and another choice was to move to The Villages, Florida after we completed the house project in Mexico.

Jim chose to stay in Mexico and I could no longer accept his huge ego and drinking which he never did before.

On my last trip from Scottsdale back to Mexico, I had a dream. I was sitting in a reception area when a man looked at me, walked toward me and kissed me on the cheek. A beautiful female voice said, "He likes you." I said, "No, he doesn't." The scene changed, I was in space and a man dressed in a hooded sweat shirt put his arms around me from behind, but I felt the most love and warmth I had not felt in a long time. The female voice said, "Compare how you feel now and how Jim makes you feel." My words were, "Yuck," with a cold and lonely feeling coming over me. Of course, this was a spiritual message, but I chose to get in my car and head back to Mexico knowing better.

I drove to Yuma, stopped for an oil change and when I was ready to leave, the car would not go into gear. What happened? When I was able to put the car in gear and drive, I stopped at some friend's house and the car stopped again. When I told them the story, both said at the same time, "You are not meant to go back to Mexico." Those friends were not spiritual in anyway. Another message!

I had the car towed to the dealership and was informed it would take a week for repairs. I had perishables in the car and the temperature outside was 110 degrees so I called Jim to come get me. He flatly told me NO. I realized then the spirit world was doing everything in hopes I would get the message! What was I to do? I needed to sell the house and that concerned me. Also knew I had to get back on *my* path...not *our path* any longer.

Returning to San Felipe I moved into the casita and had little contact with Jim. I kept asking the universe to help me sell the house so I could move on. On the third morning Jim asked my plans and I said, "I am leaving as soon as the house is finished and I will have to trust you to sell it." He replied, "Okay," and left for the office. Within twenty minutes he returned with a cash offer on the house and we needed to be out in thirty days. It was the most profound action from the universe I ever witnessed. Wow, thank you God.

I had made the right decision, but what I didn't realize until much later, the universe helped me financially by selling the house at such a profit to sustain me for many years. I think that was a nice reward since I messed up the lotto ticket so many years earlier.

Months after I left, I couldn't help wonder why we had been together, so close, loving and I thought we were meant to be together forever. Then the spirit world answered my questions.

1. I was paying back *karma*. My husband Billy was put in my life to help me through my illness. And, I was put in Jim's life to help him through his illness, thereby, I fulfilled my *karma*.
2. Jim was put in my life for an opportunity to change his life from his previous lifestyle. But he chose to go back to that lifestyle, and that is why 'our' path of destiny was to change.
3. To experience what *love* is not.

127

It was also explained to me about my past relationships. My marriages were lessons on my journey. The first marriage was to experience 'motherhood'. My second marriage was to experience 'business and finance' as I only completed the tenth grade. The third marriage was to experience 'nurturing' when I was ill.

These explanations helped me understand more about my past and how it is connected to my spiritual journey and what might lie ahead in my future.

The Warning

I had always wanted to live in Fountain Hills, Arizona, but at one time spirit said, "You are not to live in Fountain Hills," which I had forgotten. But I thought it was just when I was with Jim. I didn't think it meant never. But I moved from Scottsdale to Fountain Hills not remembering that important message. A couple of weeks after moving, the *voice within* specifically said what I was to do and not to do.

1.   Do not let Jim come to see you.
2.   Do not go anywhere with Jim.
3.   You will be in a car crash.

I didn't pay much attention to the warning regarding Jim, but was concerned about a car crash. I had a feeling I might be T-boned in an intersection, so I was very cautious when driving.

A couple weeks later Jim called and asked to come see me. I said, "Okay," as I felt I had nothing to be concerned about and was not heeding the warning.

We were happy to see each other and appeared we could just be friends. He was on his way to New

Mexico and asked to stay over-night as he had an appointment the next day before leaving, and asked if would I go with him. I agreed, and said before his appointment I had to stop by the condo as I had a buyer for it.

After leaving the condo I drove down Scottsdale Road to a restaurant for breakfast. As I turned into the parking lot a car coming out didn't give me enough room and my right rear tire hit the curb driving in. I was almost at a stop when my car raced forward, on its own, becoming airborne over some bushes, made a sharp turn, while off the ground, flew between two cars and we hit head-on into a steel and concrete pole. The air bags did not deploy; the seat belt did not hold me; my head hit the top of the windshield causing a concussion and my chest hit the steering wheel causing a fractured sternum. I was taken by ambulance to the hospital in severe pain and Jim only bruised a finger. Why, why didn't I listen or remember how 'spirit' warned me! Spirit also guided the crash as the parking lot was full of people and cars, and the only open space in the lot was where we hit the steel pole. The police said I must have hit the gas instead of the brake. I tried to explain the back tire hit the curb and caused the computer to go haywire and how the car took off at such a high speed. Little did they know that I knew something about cars since I did light stunt driving in the movie industry.

I did file a law suit against Ford and it took twelve years before they issued a 'recall' for the computer problem. And, they didn't settle my law suit!

With every injury or illness, it always created severe pain, and my arms and legs were difficult to move. This was the worst time! I could barely lift my arms high enough to feed myself and could not shampoo or comb my hair, or bend my arms to get dressed. I had to create ways to put my clothes on. I had acupuncture, TBM treatments, an MRA and MRI's, was in a hyperbaric chamber, had mini stokes, but nothing seemed to improve my condition. This was another condition that took four years to recuperate. I have no idea why each major health issue took four years before I was well again. I asked the spirit world why I had so many health issues and challenges. The spirit world answered, "Jesus didn't have it easy, did he?" And, there was no other explanation for my life of illness and challenges.

Ten months later I purchased a townhouse back in Scottsdale where I was close to doctors and a hospital. The townhouse was forty-five years old and needed to be remodeled. I painted the walls and other work around the house to help strengthen my arms and legs to get back in shape. I had new friends and neighbors and as time went on, was feeling more like myself once again.

****

Those four years were extremely challenging and now it was over, I was ready for a new man in my life. How do I go about it? At this age you didn't just go to a bar to find someone, so it was suggested I use a dating site. How embarrassed I felt doing such a thing!

I signed up on a dating site and found it quite amusing and couldn't believe some of the stories. My challenge was to find someone that wasn't quite the everyday kind of guy since I had such an unusual life, and someone who could accept me for who I am.

I put my request out to the universe, and *did not* make my request *specific* enough, once again!

The dating site introduced me to Howard and on the dating site you can also compare *similar* type men to Howard. I clicked on the 'similar' tab and to my surprise, the answer came back - Howard is unique and there are no others like him! He lived on a sailboat for twenty years sailing from San Diego to Central America and lived in Panama for two years. Panama! This is where spirit suggested I go when I still lived in Mexico. He must be important on my journey!

We met a few times for coffee and became interested in each other. I invited Howard to take a trip to Tucson where we shopped, saw old town Tucson, had dinner at a nice restaurant. Later we found a hotel to stay the night. This was not pleasant as Howard got angry over small things and I didn't know why. He appeared to have a lot of suppressed anger and I had never been around angry people and wasn't sure how to handle it. I hadn't encountered anyone with his behavior, not bad but unusual. I knew spirit had a job for me, but what?

Arriving back at his home the next day, he said, "Why don't you unpack your suitcase, and live here with me?" And, without a thought I unpacked my bags and started living with Howard on my new journey. What had I done again? Yet, I knew spirit would give me those answers before long.

Howard had two distinct sides. One was kind and giving, a man who could be trusted, did not drink, smoke or take drugs. He shared his difficult times. Those times brought hate, anger, resentment and a strong anger toward God. His health issues were heart problems and COPD.

Finally, the spirit world informed me why I was put in Howard's life. My job was to heal his health issues, help him to forgive himself and others, and most important to bring God back into his life.

My gifts of spiritualism or the healing power that God gifted me were not discussed with Howard in the beginning. However, friends learned of my gifts and made comments in front of Howard. He wanted to know more and became very interested, much to my surprise. He wanted me to give readings and help heal those that needed assistance, and all the time, I silently worked on Howard's body, mind and heart to be healed.

Howard was a veteran and had periodic doctor appointments at the VA Hospital. Almost two years of living together, he had one of his usual check-ups. The first doctor checked his heart and blood pressure and said he was very pleased, didn't know what Howard was doing, but to keep it up and cut all of his medications in half. Another doctor was to check his COPD. This was only the second time Howard had seen this doctor, and explained he had been diagnosed twenty years ago with COPD by several doctors in the VA. The doctor sternly said, "Well, you don't have COPD!" Howard did make the mistake of pointing his finger at me and said, "She healed me." The doctor was very agitated and said, "That would be a miracle, and I don't believe in miracles." That brought out Howard's aggressive personality and the two of them argued. I had to jump in to quiet both of them down.

134

Thankfully, Howard was no longer troubled with COPD. Howard never realized he was in full recovery until the doctor confirmed it. He began to question me as he had no clue anything was transpiring within his body, and I explained the best I could. Then Howard broadcast to everyone his good health and how it occurred. However, I always wanted to keep my gifts in a low profile.

On Easter Sunday, we invited several friends for a patio party. During the party Howard announced my gift of healing. My friend Pam already knew of my gift and knew my gift was used *only* when the spirit world instructed me to do so OR if someone asked me personally to be healed. Pam turned to her husband and said, "Angelo, ask Rehel for a healing," as Angelo was scheduled the next week for a pacemaker and was very apprehensive. After much coaxing from Pam, Angelo said, "Rehel, will you heal me?" I stood behind Angelo, put my hands on his shoulders and instantly Angelo got his healing. Not from me, but God! The next day Pam called while at the doctor's office and said Angelo did not need a pacemaker after all and his heart was okay. What a wonderful confirmation for an instant healing from God! Angelo has not had a problem since and that was many years ago.

To shorten this story, I made the decision to leave Howard as the stress of living together was taking a toll on my emotions and health. I also felt I had failed my spiritual directive. Howard's heart and COPD had been healed, but I was unable to bring him back to God.

Going Forward

While living with Howard, we took a trip to Panama which I loved. After we separated, I still had my home in Scottsdale and decided to sell it, go to Panama and start a new life as spirit had suggested when I was in Mexico. This would have been nice, but again, I put a kink in the plan.

I would sell my house as a 'turn-key' property. That way I would not be straddled with any furniture or contents, and put my car in storage. That way I would have a car when I returned for a visit.

The plan quickly changed as I decided to buy another house before I left. I looked at my decision as a new investment and storage for my car. However, I had one major stipulation. The deal had to be completed in six days, move in on the sixth day because I was leaving for Panama on the seventh day. I knew this was impossible as it takes ten days just for inspections. Boy was I wrong. The realtor made everything happen and I was moved in on the sixth day!

Realizing I had no furniture or contents to furnish the house for my rental investment, I canceled my plan for Panama. It took me from the middle of March to the middle of May before the project was finished. Now, I was ready for a lady's day out to celebrate and say goodbye as I was on my way to Panama.

Unfortunately, that did not happen. I was so sick the fun day was canceled and too sick to see the doctor. Once I saw several doctors, none could give me a diagnosis, and I was in this condition for a few months. I came down with the H1N1 virus and shortly after recovering from that I came down with Valley Fever, which is almost as debilitating. My stress level sky rocketed and the pain and difficulty moving my arms and legs were there once again. One specialist doctor finally found and diagnosed the problem. I was diagnosed with PMR, which is Polymyalgia Rheumatica. This disease is usually caused by stress and generally attacks white females over the age of seventy, and the medication prescribed is prednisone, which is not good for the body. Learning the cause of the disease, I immediately decided to go to Panama. My doctor felt I was making a huge mistake, but I just didn't care. I knew I could turn this condition around. The house was going to be vacant; I was going to Panama and whatever happens will happen. It was not important!

My friend, Larry who lived in Panama for several years, picked me up at the airport and took me to the wonderful 17th floor condo I had rented right on the beach in Coronado, Panama. I walked three miles on the black and white sandy beach every day and in two weeks all of the pain and symptoms of PMR had disappeared. I had made the right choice!

Spirit Messages

All the months in Arizona being so ill I did not receive any messages or guidance from the spirit world. I didn't hear the *voice within* or see any *visions*. Perhaps it took more energy than I had in my body to receive any communication. When I don't receive messages or guidance, I call it the "Void".

Five weeks after arriving in Panama I was informed that Dan, my friend Sandy's significant other had passed away. The first time I met Dan and gave him a hug, I knew he would pass away in three years. Of course, I didn't tell anyone. He knew of my gifts and sometimes would ask if he would die of a heart attack, and I told him no, which was the truth. He died of complication from cancer.

I sent my condolences and a week after Dan passed away Dan *appeared* to me from the *other side.* He asked if I would invite Sandy to Panama. He wanted her to see how much he enjoyed Panama while living on his sail boat. He wanted her to experience the blue ocean, the tropics and the beautiful black and white sandy beaches. His request was so clear I did not hesitate to contact Sandy.

I did not tell her Dan contacted me, but merely stated she might like a change of scenery during this difficult time. She jumped at the invitation, and I made arrangements for her to stay two months in the same condo building I was in.

Sandy arrived two weeks later and each day we walked the beach talking about the past, our future, and explored places, restaurants, clubs and villages throughout Panama. I finally told her how Dan had appeared to me and wanted her to see Panama, which brought on buckets of tears.

Another beautiful tropical day Sandy and I drove to Boquete to see Larry, and after our visit, we would drive to the Costa Rican border and check out what is needed to cross one border into another border and back again. Another new adventure!

That evening in Larry's home, which is in the cool highlands of Boquete, not far from the Costa Rican border, we were playing our favorite game of Mexican Train, when Dan appeared. Larry knew instantly what was happening and quickly went outside so Sandy would have her special communication with Dan.

Sandy had never seen me in a trance state and didn't know I was a channel. She only knew I gave short readings, did numerology and had done some healing work.

Dan came through and gave her some wonderful information. He answered many questions she had on her mind, and gave her information regarding her future. And, he told her he would be her guardian angel whenever she needed him.

A couple years before Dan's death, Sandy had attended one of my spiritual gatherings. After the meeting, I gave Sandy a reading telling her she would meet and marry a wonderful man named George with brown hair, and Dan would be happy for her. Sandy was so angry, she said she wouldn't ever leave Dan, and didn't want to hear anymore from me.

.   After this encounter with Dan and the spirit world, I felt the energy and messages would be coming again. It was rare that loved ones from the other side communicated with me, but a few weeks later, as Larry and I sat on the patio of my 17th floor condo, Larry asked me if I could see anything in his future, when his mother immediately jumped in. She had passed away the year before and wanted somehow to communicate with him. This communication flowed with tears and love from her to Larry and back again. I was very grateful the 'void' period was finally over after all those months!

Note: Five years later, the reading I had given Sandy came true. She moved to Florida, met George with the brown hair, got married and is happier than ever living in Ohio. She did remember the reading I gave her and was no longer angry and knew Dan was with her

***

Every day Sandy and I walked the three miles of black and white sandy beach enjoying an occasional person or some fishermen bringing in their early morning catch of fresh fish. Our conversations were mostly of the spirit world, what we might plan for our future. Now single ladies, we could do whatever we decided.

While walking back one day, instantly I was given a vision. I received no *voice* or *thought* with this new message, but was a *vision* of symbols. I saw a large dining table with all kinds of delicious food, and placed on the table was a golden/brown turkey. I knew this message meant I would receive the next important message at Thanksgiving time. It was only July and I didn't want to wait another four months… but I knew I had to be patient.

At the end of Sandy's two months stay, she went back to Arizona and I would not return to Arizona until late October and I was not receiving any more messages.

My original plan was to lease my home in Arizona and live permanently in Panama. However, after living in Panama all those months, I decided it was not the place for me as I desired to return to my spiritual gifts, perhaps meet a new man to share life with, and I didn't see those opportunities in Panama. So, at the end of my stay, I returned to Arizona.

****

It was two days before Thanksgiving and the *voice within* came to me, and instructed me to go to The Villages, Florida! It brought back a message I received in Mexico when spirit gave me the choices of going to Panama and The Villages, Florida. I had completed Panama and now was being instructed to go to Florida. This was all part of my spiritual journey.

While in Panama I met a lovely couple from The Villages. They invited me to visit and thought I would love it there. As soon as I received the message from spirit to go to The Villages, I invited Sandy and contacted the couple. I informed them we would stay in a hotel for a week, but she said that would be too expensive and would call me back. She found a villa for rent with two bedrooms and we could stay six weeks for less money than a stay in the hotel. How could I refuse!

144

Sandy and I jumped on the plane the day after Thanksgiving, flew to Orlando where we were shuttled to our villa in The Villages. The new friends took us under their wings, and showed us everything. However, as much as we enjoyed the new adventure, both of us did not feel at home in The Villages. We concluded neither of us would return once we left on New Year's Day.

We were excited to be back in Arizona and looked forward to making plans for our futures.

I was home less than a week when I received a very strong message from the spirit world, which said, "You are to sell your home, get rid of everything you have from your past and move to The Villages, Florida." There was also a *strong insight* that I was to live there from May 15th until mid to late December at which time I would receive further instructions.

With a strong message, I like to wait until I receive the same message two or three times before I take action. The message did repeat itself and I had to accomplish those important instructions. I called a realtor, put the house up for sale and I would eliminate all contents from my past to move forward on my journey.

A few days after receiving the first message, a second message was very clear, "You are to write a book, and do it quickly." I had never written a book and didn't know what to write.

My friend Pam was working on her spiritual journey, and was overwhelmed with it. I suggested she let everything go and get back to it when she was ready. The very next day she called excited to tell me she had a message for me. Her spirit message said, "Rehel is to write a book and the title is "A How to Guide, Listen to the Voice Within'. This would be a book to teach beginners how to start on their spiritual journey.

As I pondered what to write sitting in front of my computer, my fingers took off as if I were doing automatic writing. I let my fingers take over and typed all of the thoughts and messages that were delivered to me. I typed until the messages would stop. At times I was directed to get information from the internet to be written in the book. When I attempted to write on Sunday, a message said it was a day of rest and a holy day, and to begin again on Monday. Within three weeks and a few short hours of writing the book was finished.

The book was ready to be published, but I had no idea how to get it published. I wanted a message or a sign to direct me. As I sat at the computer, I asked for guidance when a pop-up regarding a publisher appeared. I knew it was the sign I asked for. The pop-up stated I could 'live chat' with someone. I felt intimidated and not sure what to say, when the *voice* spoke, "What do you have to lose?" I put my question to the 'live chat' and the response was that someone would call me on a phone line. Within ten minutes of discussion, I had a publisher and the book would be released and available at the same time I would arrive in The Villages.

My home had not been sold and it became a concern, but decided to move to The Villages as directed regardless. I leased a beautiful home on the golf course with a magnificent view. It was now April and there was so much to do before May 15th. I wanted to make sure everything was in order before moving, including my yearly physical, dentist, car serviced and anything to be completed before the trip.

As I was driving to keep an appointment with my eye doctor, I got very angry with the spirit world and said, "I have done everything you wanted me to do and there is no buyer for my house, what is the problem? You said it would be sold. So, if you want me to sell the house you better bring me a buyer!" I felt badly and doubted the messages I had received months ago, yet I felt I needed to continue on this journey.

Arriving home late, the house was quite dark, I turned on the kitchen lights and on the counter was a card indicating a possible buyer. The very next day I had a solid contract from a buyer in Illinois that didn't even see the house! They saw it on a 'virtual tour' on their computer. Not only that, but the new buyer had the same exact address in Illinois as my old house in Scottsdale! Was this a coincidence? My doubting came to an end and knew the spirit world was directing my steps on my new spiritual journey.

The sale was a 'turn-key' investment for the buyer, which helped me eliminate all of my belongings from my past and anything left I donated to the veterans. Once this was done, all I had left was my car, a few clothes, a few books, photos and computer. I was doing my best to fulfill my directive.

On May 10th I was ready to start my journey from Arizona to Florida. Larry did not want me to travel alone and flew from Panama to Arizona to make sure I was safe. We had a great time traveling all the different states and arrived in The Villages on May 15th right on schedule.

****

Larry and I drove straight to the beautiful home I would be staying until December. The next morning when I opened the front door, there was my *new published book*! I had accomplished every tasks spirit directed me to do. Anxiously wanted to know more of what was next on my continued journey.

The Villages is a huge senior community over 130,000 people, with everything you could think of to do. There are many highly evolved spiritual people, so felt I was directed to the right area to continue whatever was in store for me.

I got emerged in meditation, healings, dowsing, parapsychology, UFO'S, drumming, astrology and more. I met a lot of people and formed a close relationship with a lady. We shared a lot and did the 'normal' things besides all the spiritual stuff, so I had a good balance in life.

Time forged ahead and I was in the 'void' period once again! I was concerned where I was to go at the end of the year, but no response from the spirit world. I bothered them so much they finally gave me an answer.

"It is helpful to understand what is for you, but you must listen to the voice within whenever this is available. It is not now to know that answer as there are many things in store for you. But, don't be surprised how it comes about. Not ask, but receive. Time will tell."

I immediately asked, "Anything else? What do you want me to know?" This is the answer to my questions.

"It is time to be *expectful*, but use the knowledge coming to you to further your gain and prosperity. Use it to enhance your answers and give it time to process. Give it a limited time of 3 to 4 months then you can make your own decision how you must take your next journey of hope, wisdom and welfare. It is a time of excitement. Don't stress or lose your mental facilities of depression. Stay in abundance and we will help in those down moments. Be not a child, but a huge child of wisdom and of God. Be now blessed and go forward with your connection to God and let all the worries go. I know it is not easy, but just do it my dear."

I knew this message meant my mission was to take each day one at a time and not make any plans or decisions until the next directive in December.

After the time of receiving this message, I went about my daily life. I had the opportunity to speak at meetings, gave a few readings and assisted in healings. I also had fun going to parties, dinner, dancing and meeting interesting people. I also had a book signing at Barnes and Noble for my new book.

An interesting change was about to take place. My new lady friend and I went dancing and on this particular night we watched a gentleman walk into the dance club. He had an unusual aura about him and everyone seemed to notice him. He walked in and stood next to me then asked me to dance.

This is 'our' story as we *listened to the voice within* and compared our notes.

****

Mack, his name, is a religious and spiritual person and is also guided by the 'voice within'. This is what he related to me after we became better friends.

When I stood by you, I thought about asking you to dance, but thought you wouldn't dance with me. And, when I had that thought, the 'voice within' said, "Ask her to dance." Again, thought you wouldn't dance with me, but the 'voice within' kept repeating "Ask her to dance." After the third time, I asked you to dance and you accepted. It was a slow tune, and as soon as my arms went around you, I felt we became one!

And, I felt the same thing! Wow!

As we became closer, we compared all of our similarities. Here is a list of those similarities.

I was guided to move to The Villages on May 15th. Mack was guided to move to The Villages on May 18th. My birthday day is October 14th and his birthday is October 18th. We both drive 'red' SUV's and love to dance.

We compared family backgrounds. My mother passed away at age 47 and Mack's father passed away at age 47. My brother was killed at age 33 and his brother was killed at age 33. Mack's ex-wife died in a car accident after a seizure. My dearest friend, Lincoln died after a seizure; my grandmother's name was Ella and Mack's mother's name is Ella. My father had dementia and his mother has onset dementia.

We compared our physical injuries and health issues, which were almost identical. We kept track of other coincidences happening in our daily lives.

My friend and I went to a meeting where 'Men in Black' was the theme. Mack had left town to attend a costume party, where he and his friend dressed as 'Men in Black'. Neither one of us knew.

We spoke of our similarities and were concerned 'why' we had met, but also knew it was not a lasting relationship. We also knew our differences were greater than our similarities.

****

In an earlier message spirit had said to wait 3 to 4 months before making decisions of hope, wisdom and welfare on my next journey, but I was still in the 'void' period. And, in September spirit said, "Much has transpired since we talked and there is more to come, but wait for the answers and comply with our suggestions about your living quarters."

In October the 'Void' period was over. I was receiving messages about many different things, but was not receiving any guidance for my personal life. I took it upon myself where my new journey was to take me without waiting for a direct message. Wrong decision!

I decided to buy a house, I was preapproved for a loan in fifteen minutes and the closing would be on December 15th. Everything happened so fast, forgetting spirit had instructed me to live each day and wait for the next directive. Spirit did not say, have a relationship with a man or buy a house. I created a different plan for myself thinking it would be okay.

Finally, realizing I had made so many mistakes, I wanted to correct what I had done. I canceled the purchase contract on the house. I ended my relationship with Mack, and later learned from spirit why we were together; it was to heal both of us from a past life.

Since I had made all the wrong choices once again, I knew I would be in for some challenges, which was always the case. My angels and guides were not happy with me. My real lesson was to learn PATIENCE!

The message from spirit was, "Congratulations on departing from your previous intentions. Take time to figure out what you have done and be glad you came to that conclusion."

Many things changed after that. I had no guidance at all. I didn't know where to move or what to do. I was now in the 'Void Challenge', so I had to make my own choices not knowing if they were right or wrong. The home I had rented until late December was rented to someone else and I had to move. I rented a small villa for one month, and decided to go to Panama until April, and then return to the same beautiful rental in The Villages where I started.

With all of the challenging experiences while in Panama, I learned a *different* form of spiritualism. It was a form of 'manifestation' unlike anything I had experienced. An example: If I made a negative statement, true or false, it manifested immediately. That was very disturbing. Another example: I spoke to a lady about the lack of rain in Panama. There were no clouds in the sky or any indication of rain and within a few minutes it poured rain for about twenty minutes, and did not rain again all the time I was in Panama. Also, when driving on the Pan American highway I commented to my friend that I had seen an Iguana cross the road the last time I was on the highway. In less than two minutes an Iguana ran across the road right in front of us. These experiences manifested whenever I made such statements.

I wondered if I was able to manifest these things, then why was I not able to manifest things I would like to experience or have in my life? But there was no answer for me.

With all of this new manifestation experience, I was still in the 'Void Challenge' with no guidance, and unsure of my decisions, but paid special attention to any intuition or feelings I might have.

****

Now back in the beautiful house on the golf course in The Villages, I waited for new messages and instructions. One day my landlady informed me the

155

house had been rented to someone for one week in September, and I could stay at her condo in Cocoa Beach for that week. That made no sense to me. Why move all of my belongings for just one week? This was definitely a 'sign' a change was coming.

My friend Sandy was moving to Florida from Arizona, so I decided to check out the area where she would be living as a possibility for me to live there too.

I invited a friend to go on the trip of adventure. Indeed, it was a trip of adventure! All of my spirituality returned! What fun we were having listening to all of the messages and synchronicities. It was coming so fast we could barely keep up with it, which made us laugh and have more fun than we had in a long time. The best part, I 'knew' what I was to do in my future.

I wasn't getting direct messages but my intuition was very strong and guiding me what to do. I was to purchase a home in The Villages and stay two years. I put the plan in order and the right house appeared and everything I needed fell into place as my journey started once again.

The very first time I arrived in The Villages, I attended a UFO group and spoke of my experiences with my space brothers, also how I commanded them to leave me alone. During the meeting a lady asked why I didn't try to communicate with them again. In all those years I never thought about it. I took her comment seriously and for the next three years I asked for the space brothers to communicate with me again, until one day this is what they communicated to me.

"Oh dear, long time no see and we feel we will have a new start again."

I asked, "Is this you the space brothers?"

They replied, "Oh well, if you want to call us that. We are everywhere conducting business along the way. We are entrenched with you while you give your short speaks at so called meetings of space beings that we see you attend. It is fine to go there and not all statements are true, but you are living proof it has transpired. We like that you contacted us again. I am part of 'Desca' that you spoke about, but in the beginning, we will not use any formalities to contact you. Listen carefully when we do talk to you as our speaking will be different than your 'entity' groups you communicate with. And, we will adjust our speaking for you."

Note: 'Desca' was the space alien George Van Tassel communicated with in the 50's

I have continued communications with my space brothers since that time. I have been informed about the universe, politics, climate conditions, currents events and more. I am in contact with them most of the time and they keep me updated on world events.

I joined more spiritual groups and began channeling as I had done in the 80's. Shortly after, I was told to write all messages instead of verbal channeling and whom to share the messages with.

I am a strong believer in God, his angels and guides. I feel His messages are very profound. They always guide me on my path to enlightenment.

Here is an excerpt from one of God's messages:

- God decided to create a human being and imposed new standards on mankind. God created man with free will and man went astray following his own set of rules; made havoc on the planet. God let the world of humans be destroyed by the flood. Then mankind started anew again and only temporarily favored God's set of rules, but went astray again. So, as time went on, He brought forth a son (Jesus Christ) to be worshiped. This did begin to change man back to where God wanted man to follow His rules and once again man declined to be a better person. Now what will God do with the chaotic fashion that man has produced from all the centuries of free will! With God's new plan, all will not have free will. All will have an understanding of Love, Compassion, Strength, Forgiveness and all will cooperate for His sake.

The messages I received from God through His angels, are different from the messages I receive from my guides, masters, entities or space brothers. All of these messages are teaching me about my life's journey.

****

After living in my home for almost two years I was directed to move out of The Village to a home in Summerfield, Florida only a few miles away. Spirit informed me the house I was living in was very detrimental to my health. At night I could feel a vibration in the master bedroom and began sleeping in the guest bedroom. I found the only place I could sleep was on the living room couch. The vibration continued and got worse each day. I had the house checked and was told it might be the sewer system, some thought it was from the new electric smart meters that were installed. Spirit said the house was interfering with my energy frequency and I must move.

However, I was informed before moving, another Soul Transference of the 'second kind' would take place. Right away I could feel the changes and knew it would take approximately fourteen days before the transference would be completed, and I looked forward to the new changes on my journey.

Once I settled into my new home, my journey took more twists, turns and changes in my spiritualism which I had not encountered before. I had feelings and unexplainable thoughts and when I asked spirit about those feelings and thoughts, spirit replied I was having **another** 'Soul Transference', to relax and not worry 'who' the new 'soul' might be. What happened? Did the new 'soul' that took over my body fourteen days ago not like this body and left, and that's why another new 'soul' was being transferred into me?   I had so many questions.

With the 'newest soul' now entering my body all the previous memories were being reviewed. Why was I seeing those memories? I had no attachment to them! Spirit simply said the past memories would not be in my memory much longer and the new process would continue for some time.

One day sitting in the living room I felt it was time for lunch. When I went into the kitchen, I was surprised my lunch had not manifested. I was confused. My thoughts were – wow, I have to use this body to make lunch, and when I tried to take a lid off a bottle, it didn't just manifest from my thoughts. Again, I thought it was so hard to use this body to get anything done. I thought I could clean the house by manifesting it and it just didn't work. I questioned everything and thought how difficult it is to be a human. I felt like an extraterrestrial and not a human anymore.

The heritage of DeAnne's original body and soul was English and Danish, and after I went through the first 'soul transference' of the second kind, I was curious about any differences. I took a DNA test and the results reported I was Sub-Saharan African and Austrian, which would make me black and this body is very light skinned. Could it have been a mistake? Once this new soul transference was complete, I would like another DNA test to see if there are more differences.

A couple of months earlier a group of us went to see a channel. She chose me out of a large crowd and said to me, "When you pass on, Jesus will take your hand and no others will be there." Next, she said, "You are from the 6th dimension and you are 'part' E.T.

I believed her and now I had a better understanding what was happening to my body and my mind. This would be another new experience on my life path.

At times I was living a 'parallel life, if there is such a thing. I had my daily/normal life and at the same time I could see another dimension. I was with other people, knew their names, and had conversations with them. I would ask where they were from, what they were doing, what locations and countries we were in. I knew their phone numbers and some said they were attending a conference. While this was happening, simultaneously I wrote down names, phone numbers, countries, locations, and even the name of the building the conference was being held. The next day I would research the countries, locations, call phone numbers, and found the conference location. And, being shocked says it mildly.... everything I researched was confirmed! I understood how everything is connected to the next person or event in life. My question was; do we live parallel lives simultaneously? Maybe! However, I *was* having that experience or what else could it be?

I had developed several health issues while living in the house in The Villages and I sought out a 'functional' medicine doctor for help. He wanted me to have the mercury and any other metals removed from my teeth as my body had very high levels of metal toxicity. He referred me to a holistic dentist for this procedure. What a gifted dentist! We became instant friends and after some time, she learned I was a medium and felt she could share her extraterrestrial experience with me.

She had two patients, male and female, very tall, slim, came in for work on their teeth, however, she did not tell me what they wanted done. She said when she was to inject the anesthesia into their gums, she could not find a bone. She informed them that it would be very painful without anesthesia, and they said it would not be painful and to please do the procedure. The more they got acquainted she asked more questions of them. They informed her they were E.T.'s. They were not from a planet but came from a star and they were 200 years old. They were on earth going to many places to evaluate earth and human conditions. She saw them twice more and have not heard from them since. She would love for them to come back.

I also met a gentleman who is fairly well known from England now living in Florida. He has been with two E.T.'s constantly since he was eight years old. His stories with the E.T.' have been astounding. He wrote a book of his experiences, which he gave me. In the back of the book, he had a sketch of the two E.T.'s that are with him, and I showed my dentist the sketch. The dentist and her staff were shocked!! The sketch was identical to the male and female E.T patients that were in her office. Now, this gentleman and the dentist are going to compare their notes. It is interesting that the dentist and this man live in communities not far from each other so they can talk about their mutual E.T. friends. Was this meant to be? Probably, and you can see how we are all connected!

The dentist and her husband invited me on a trip to Miami to see a 'psychic reader'. Tom, my mentor, and Henrietta from the past, were the only ones that could read me. I mentioned this to the dentist, however, said it would be fun to have a reading anyway.

The reader is quite famous and the first thing he said to me was, "Nobody can read you, can they?" I knew he was on the right track. It was a great reading, and as he read, he asked if I was interested in E.T.'s. He told me in September an E.T. would come from Atlantis and the Pleiades to give me a message. I wondered if this would be the message, **"It's time?"** instead of the previous messages the space brothers gave me when they said, **"It's almost time."** How exciting that would be to get an updated message from our space brothers.

****

164

My life was expanding with more new experiences. The spirit world had more instructions and sometimes I had no idea why or what it meant, but I complied when asked.

First, I was to look into people's eyes that were blue. Was I learning about their souls? It was troubling to look into the blue eyes, but it wasn't all blue eyes that were troubling. After that, I was to look into eyes that were more of a golden color. When I did, it gave me an uncomfortable feeling. I was not directed to look into any eyes of a different color. Then I was directed to listen to the sound of voices. The spirit world must have done something to my hearing as most voice sounds are extremely irritating. Could this be a lesson in different vibrations? The majority of irritation came from females. They sounded high pitched, whinny, nasal with a low gravel tone. I immediately had to turn away and if it came from the TV, I turned the sound off right away as it was too irritating for me to listen to. And, as of today those sounds are still bothering me.

I was very aware of the different changes I was going through. When I looked at people in person or on TV, I would say in my mind, "Why are they so ugly or why do they make themselves look so ugly?" I equated this to humans looking at aliens, thinking aliens are ugly. But now I felt like an alien looking at humans thinking they were so ugly. However, interestingly it didn't happen with the people I knew. I had no clue what was happening or what was I to learn.

Also, when I listened to people telling their emotional stories, I could not understand why anyone would have those emotions. While watching a movie on TV or the news, I didn't understand the emotions that were displayed and asked why do humans do that?

I felt like two different people – alien and human. The human part of me understood everything, while the alien part of me made no sense as to why humans did such things. What a strange journey I was going through. I began to wonder if I was mentally disturbed, or having a nervous breakdown as I couldn't understand, and had so many questions.

After a few months, the new soul was seeded in, which took longer than the fourteen days as it did before. I was feeling more like myself or more normal you might say. I had no more strange directives from the spirit world. But I continued on my journey receiving messages from the space brothers and the spirit world. And, as directed I have kept a record of all those messages, perhaps to be shared in another book.

My intuition was very strong and even the simplest urges and insights were there to act upon. I loved it when I would think of something and instantly was given an answer. Or, was given signs and clues to carry out and what those signs were telling me to do. It was like a new spiritual game, right down to telling me what I was to eat for dinner. How interesting and what fun for a change. Perhaps this leads to other events on my journey to enlightenment!

I keep asking the E.T.'s and the spirit world all these questions and to please tell me why my life has been so unusual and what am I to do with these experiences and information. Will it help anyone else on their journey in life? Was it just for my own destiny and enlightenment? Was it as the wise Indians told me, I was simply to 'touch' lives? Was that it? I want to know!

Fortunately, I have my friend Larry that listens to all my concerns, but can't explain it any more than I can.

My story is an **UNEXPLAINED MYSTERY!**

***

This is my spiritual journey. Hopefully you will be able to have a great spiritual journey. And, if some of you have similar experiences, know that you are not crazy, but simply on your spiritual path. Most people may not understand your journey and that is okay!

I hope my experiences helped you in some way and that you have a better understanding of what you are capable of as you continue on your journey to enlightenment!

This is not the End,

But a Continued Spiritual Journey

Dear reader, I would love it if you would post an honest review on Amazon about this book.

Thank you and sparkle on!

My Books:

*The second book is a republishing of the first book.

A How to Guide – Listening to the Voice Within

Listen to the Voice Within – A Spiritual Journey

Made in the USA
Middletown, DE
09 December 2022

17839554R00106